Hope for t

Contemporary Values
of the Restoration Movement

HOPE INTERNATIONAL
UNIVERSITY PRESS

Table of Contents

1

Hope International University began as Pacific Bible Seminary in 1928. The first graduating class was two men. One became a pastor. The other became a businessman. That beginning set the tone for HIU to stress the 'priesthood of all believers'. We have and we do educate all of our students to be ministers wherever they may find themselves. One's ministry is where one is. Therefore, we wish to educate our students in a chosen field of endeavor, but to do so with ministry in mind.

Whether for one's occupational skill or one's personal spiritual development, Hope educates students to read, write, think and speak. A major method to reach this goal is through critical thinking. Hope wants her students to be able to assess and process the information they access through classes, books, personal discussions and experience.

Our heritage is commonly called the Stone-Campbell Movement or the Restoration Movement. Some have called our background the 19th Century Reformation. The original leaders: Thomas and Alexander Campbell, Barton W. Stone, Raccoon John Smith and others believed the body of Christ had become too denominated. The Campbells were members of the Old Light Anti-Burgher Seceder Presbyterian Church. Stone came from a Baptist background. Their desire was to see unity in the church rather than division. They built their movement upon such sayings as:

"We are not the only Christians, but we are Christians only!"
"Where the Bible speaks, we speak. Where the Bible is silent, we are silent."
"No Creed but Christ. No Book but the Bible."
"In essentials, Unity. In non-essentials, Liberty. In all things, Love."

They decided to call themselves Christians or Disciples of Christ for that is what they were. Whether one is a Baptist, Methodist, Lutheran, or Catholic, one is a Christian. The terms Christian and Disciple of Christ unite believers rather than divide them.

This book is not a history of those people or that movement. Rather, the concepts they stressed that are most important. This book explains many of the values of the Stone-Campbell Movement as they apply to today's church. We hope these articles written by professors of Hope International University will bring hopeful values to churches today. We believe these values can transform the church to truly make an impact upon our world. May this study enlighten and challenge you to be a faithful follower of Jesus!

Acknowledgments

A work like this is the result of many peoples' efforts. Those who have written chapters, questions and leaders' guides have drawn upon their expertise and research to present succinct, insightful concepts for you to consider. As colleagues and friends their insights are much appreciated. They are professors of Hope International University. They are scholars and they are churchmen. They have a commitment to Restoration Values.

John Webb has taken the work of these writers and edited with his eagle eye. He has helped hone and clarify our writing. He has done so willingly, professionally and in a timely fashion. His contribution is greatly appreciated.

Finally, kudos go to my Administrative Assistant, Brittany Bauman. She has taken all our efforts and formatted them into this book. Her hours of contacting and compiling the professors' chapters has expedited the publication of this volume. May her legion be many!!

Joe Grana

Contributors

Introduction – Derry, John, President – Lincoln Christian College, B.A.; Lincoln Christian Seminary, M.A.; Western Illinois University, M.S.; East Tennessee State University, Ed.D.

1. Lordship of Christ – Richardson, Steve, Associate Professor of Biblical Studies – Northwest Christian College, B.Th.; Emmanuel School of Religion, M.Div,; Northwest Christian College, D.D.

2. Authority of Scripture – Webb, John, Professor, College of Ministry and Biblical Studies - Lincoln Christian College B.A.; Southern Illinois University M.S.; Lincoln Christian Seminary M.Div.; The Ohio State University, Ph.D.

3. Unity of Christians – Matson, David, Associate Professor of Biblical Studies – Hope International University B.A.,; Pepperdine University, M.A.; Baylor University, Ph.D.

4. Covenant – Sonnenberg, Gene, Retired: Adjunct Professor of Biblical Studies.- Northwest Christian College, B. Th.; Emmanuel School of Religion, M. Div.; Fuller Theological Seminary, D. Min.

5. Mission and World Evangelism – Lines, Kevin, Associate Professor of Biblical Studies – Milligan College, B.A.; Emmanuel Christian Seminary, M.A.R.; Asbury Theological Seminary, Ph. D.

6. Priesthood of All Believers – Towne, Phil, Adjunct Professor of Biblical Studies, Director of SALT – Hope International University, B.A.; Fuller Theological Seminary, M.A.; George Fox Evangelical Seminary, M.Div.; Fuller Theological Seminary, Ph. D. in progress

7. Servant Leadership – Grana, Joe, Dean of PCCMBS; Professor of Biblical Studies – Lincoln Christian College, B.A.; Hope International University, M.A.; Lincoln Christian Seminary M.Div., M.A.; University of Dubuque Theological Seminary, D.Min.

8. The Church – Richardson, K.C. – Associate Professor of Biblical Studies - Pacific Christian College, B.A.; Emmanuel School of Religion, M. Div., University of California Los Angeles, Ph.D.

9. Freedom of Interpretation – Baker, William, Professor of Biblical Studies – Lincoln Christian College, B.A.; Trinity Evangelical Divinity School, M.A., M.Div.; University of Aberdeen, Ph.D.

Hope for the Future
Introduction
Dr. John Derry

The first of Hope International University's six core values is, *"To remain Christ-centered, biblically based and focused on serving the Church while maintaining the values of the Restoration Movement."* Our heritage is found within the Christian Churches and Churches of Christ fellowship and since 1928 we have been preparing leaders who are serving in hundreds of these congregations, missions, and parachurch ministries around the world. Today we continue to emphasize that the university belongs to these churches and our responsibility is to respond to their higher education and leadership development needs. We are committed to ensuring strong ties to the churches that have made this school possible and to avoiding the path taken by many universities in America that no longer value such a relationship and are only nominally affiliated with a church constituency. This book is an example of that priority and is intended as a tool to help students and church members understand some of the principles we believe and teach.

The farther we are removed from transformational moments, the less vivid they become in our memory. Unless we continue to remind each generation of those events that have shaped our culture, we are in danger of losing the important lessons learned and of repeating mistakes of the past. In an early meeting to discuss the concept of this study guide, I looked around the table and observed that those invited to participate in writing the various sections all had adult children who were starting families of their own. Many of these young men and women have grown up in the church and may or may not know much about the history of the Restoration Movement or its key figures such as Barton W. Stone or Thomas and Alexander

Campbell. As we considered what topics to include, I commented, "We may not be able to pass on to our children an awareness of the fascinating events that took place when this movement began. However, we should be sure they understand the values that have made it what it is and that they embrace and share those values in the churches where they serve."

The word "movement" implies change and transformation. That was the motivation for church leaders Barton Stone and Thomas Campbell, both Presbyterian ministers, when they determined it was time for a change. They independently came to the same conclusion that the church of their time had allowed tradition and human creeds to divide the Body of Christ, and was imposing upon its members teachings that were inconsistent with Scripture. They began to articulate what was perceived by some to be a radical concept of unity based on the authority of the Bible. They were soon joined by believers from various denominational backgrounds. In 1809 Thomas Campbell prepared a document entitled *Declaration and Address* in which he outlined 13 propositions. By way of introduction he states, "They are merely designed for opening up the way, that we may come fairly and firmly to original ground upon clear and certain premises, and take up things just as the apostles left them; that thus disentangled from the accruing embarrassments of intervening ages, we may stand with evidence upon the same ground on which the church stood at the beginning."

The clear objective of these men was to challenge Christians to "restore the ancient order of things" pertaining to the church, using the New Testament as the divine standard. Out of this effort came what is known as the Restoration Movement. Much has transpired within this movement over the past two hundred years. In this book several references are cited to serve as resources for further research into the history, principles and growth of churches that have accepted the call of restoration.

The world changes, but the gospel message remains the same, and in every generation the church is confronted with how to most effectively serve as the "salt of the earth" and the "light of the world" without compromising that message or allowing the influences of the world to shape the church into something God never intended. It is a strong church that maintains its integrity while making the necessary adjustments to penetrate the diverse cultures of the world. And now in the 21st century, with globalization accelerating at an unparalleled pace, Christians must be all the more alert to ensuring we hold fast to the values that keep us connected to our roots. The process of restoration is ongoing and will demand constant attention to the unfinished task before the church as it strives to be all that God desires.

Lesson #1: The Lordship of Jesus Christ
Stephen Richardson

Kimberly, who confessed Jesus as the Son of God and became an obedient disciple years ago, has been visiting a church nearby. She enjoys the friendly spirit of the members, but has been increasingly troubled by one of the congregation's rules. Church by-laws forbid anyone who does not agree with the denomination's creed to share in the Lord's Supper (commonly called Communion). Creeds are written statements of sects and denominations defining their particular understanding of correct Christian teaching and practice and often are used as a test of who is to be included in the church. The congregation's leaders explain that while they do not intend to suggest one who disagrees with their creed is out of fellowship with Christ, the church is obligated to adhere strictly to its practice of close Communion. Kimberly is distressed because she cherishes her experience of Communion with fellow believers. However, she must admit she cannot accept some statements in the creed, because she believes them to be out of harmony with the Scriptures. Excluded from the Lord's Supper, she always leaves the assembly (church) feeling like an outcast from the family of God.

Thomas Campbell, an early pioneer of the 19th Century American Reformation (sometimes called the Restoration

Movement), penned one of the most profound and promising unity statements in the history of the church, the *Declaration and Address*. The first of thirteen propositions in the *Address* asserts:

> That the church of Christ upon earth is essentially, intentionally, and constitutionally one; consisting of all those in every place that *profess their faith in Christ* and *obedience to him* in all things according to the scriptures, and *that manifest the same* by their tempers and conduct, and of none else as none else can be truly and properly called Christians (emphasis added).

It is remarkable, given the religious climate in early 19th century America, that Campbell did not define a Christian in terms of denominational loyalty or agreement with a creedal statement. Instead, he considered one of any denomination a Christian who confessed faith in Jesus as Lord and gave evidence of allegiance by conforming to Christ-like character. The Lordship of Jesus Christ has been the cohesive principle of this movement from its inception, as well as the heart of its appeal to the unity of the church.

John the Apostle opened his gospel declaring that the Word of God, which in fact *was* God, ". . . became flesh and made his dwelling among us" (John 1:14). John claimed what the church has confessed ever since—God the Father has been revealed in the life of Jesus of Nazareth. When Jesus invited the needy to come to Him, God the Father was showing His loving purpose. When Jesus acted in mercy, God the Father was exposing His forgiving heart. When Jesus spoke with power, God the Father was declaring His authority.

As this good news advanced beyond the walls of Jerusalem into surrounding regions, and even to all parts of the known world, the heart of the message about Jesus was consistent. God sent Him; cruel men executed Him; but death could not hold Him. By raising Jesus from the dead, God announced He had given His Son authority over all things (Acts

2:36), a fact Jesus Himself had admitted before returning to the Father when He claimed, "All authority in heaven and on earth has been given to me" (Matthew 28:18). The Apostle Paul stated the same truth about the Lord, stating, ". . . who through the Spirit of holiness was declared with power to be the Son of God by his resurrection from the dead: Jesus Christ our Lord" (Romans 1:4).

Jesus authorized His apostles to lead the church. Because they were eyewitnesses of Jesus and received His commission, the apostles exercised authority in the Church and communicated the mind of Christ to His followers. As people submit to Jesus in obedience, they demonstrate their surrender in two significant acts. A believer's first act of obedience after acknowledging Jesus' Lordship is being *baptized into Christ.* Baptism is the believer's entry into a loving relationship with God known as a covenant (an agreement). In addition, the church gathers regularly to *share the Lord's Supper* in which disciples, uniting as one Body for worship and mission in the name of Christ Jesus, renew their pledge to be faithful to the covenant.

In light of the Lordship of Jesus Christ, the Restoration Movement has resisted two things historically found in the church. One of those is creeds. When churches understood their creeds to communicate the authority of Christ and His apostles, they looked with suspicion upon those who disagreed and often removed them from the church. While thoughts in creeds may provide valuable insight into how a denomination understands Scripture, creeds do not bear the authority of Jesus Christ and must not be used to define a faithful Christian.

We also resist the claim that the apostles' authority has been passed down to officials or leaders, known as clergy in some Christian denominations. Of course, the church must preserve and deliver to subsequent generations the witness and instruction of Christ's apostles. We simply do not believe that continuing the apostles' authority in contemporary church officials is necessary for protecting the Gospel's truth. However, we value leaders from every denomination in which the Lord has given his church. Out of their Christian maturity they offer instruction as gifts for the entire church to consider as they speak from deep faith in Christ, if not with His authority.

In fellowship with disciples worldwide, we humbly pursue understanding of Jesus' will so we can complete His mission. We are encouraged that in this day there are fewer roadblocks to churches practicing unity in the understanding and application of the Lordship of Jesus Christ.

Discussion Questions:

1. The illustration at the beginning of this essay is a true and contemporary account. Do you believe the church in the illustration is consistent when it claims not to judge one's standing with the Lord while withholding that one from the most significant act of fellowship in the church? What are some weaknesses of using particular denominational creeds to define a Christian in good standing?

2. Discuss Thomas Campbell's definition of a Christian. Do you agree with him? Why? What, if any, reservations do you have about his statement? Why is it important to make one's confession of and obedience to Christ's Lordship the priority in defining a Christian?

3. In American culture, we do not often use the words *Lord* and *Lordship* outside the church. What are some more familiar synonyms for *Lord*? How would you apply these synonyms to Jesus?

4. In what specific ways has your growing knowledge of Jesus shaped your daily decisions and relationships with others?

5. What continually comes to your mind in meditation during the Lord's Supper about your congregation's obedience to Christ's Lordship? In what ways is your congregation strong and effective in responding to Christ? How is your congregation weak in obedience and in need of repentance?

6. Your church may not have an official denominational creed but still may have long-held unwritten assumptions about certain issues that shape activity in the church. Have you ever had an experience in your church when its creed (written or unwritten) seemed to be out of step with the will of Christ or a hindrance to His mission? What is a practical wholesome way of dealing with such a contradiction?

7. In Colossians 1:28-29, Paul describes the goal of his missionary ministry. How does his statement in verse 28 relate to the issue of the Lordship of Jesus Christ?

NOTES

NOTES

NOTES

Lesson #2: The Authority of Scripture
John David Webb

Growing up in the home of a Restoration Movement (hereafter referred to as the RM) devotee and preacher, it seems the common phrases historically used must have been repeated daily, displayed on plaques and posters around the house, and resided as a part of the everyday family conversations. Or perhaps it was the years of study in a RM college and seminary and the multiple courses taken taught by a RM committed faculty, especially our beloved Seminary Dean, Enos Dowling, where these phrases were drilled into our psyches.

"Where the Scriptures speak, we speak; where the Scriptures are silent, we are silent."
"No creed but Christ, no book but the Bible, no law but love, no name but the divine."
"Call Bible things by Bible names."
"The church of Jesus Christ on earth is essentially, intentionally, and constitutionally one."
"We are Christians only, but not the only Christians."
"In essentials, unity; in opinions, liberty; in all things, love (charity)."

Though not RM originals, these propositions gave direction during the foundational time of this movement. They express key values even now.

Dr. James B. North posits that the phrases give us deep insight into the simple sounding, but difficult challenges that mark the movement. He suggests that "the Restoration Movement is built on two key concerns: the concern for the unity of all Christians in the one body of Christ, and the concern for the Bible as the only authority for the faith and practice of Christians" (North *Union in Truth* 6). In this brief essay, we consider the second principle and the value of this essay, the Bible as the sole authority of our faith and practice. (The writer will not enter into the distinctions between "authority" and "interpretation" in this document; it requires a longer, more detailed study. And though it became a battle that included the matter of the "silences" of the Bible as well, I will not jump into those deep waters here.)

The early RM arose because varied creeds had been developed by the various arms of the American Protestant world. Thomas and Alexander Campbell, both part of the Scottish Presbyterian Church, found themselves at odds over Presbyterian creeds and became a part of the Baptist Church in America. However, their spoken opposition to the creeds of their new group resulted in their ouster. Ultimately, T. Campbell's "Declaration and Address" sounded this cry, "Where the Scriptures speak, we speak; where the Scriptures are silent, we are silent." As Richardson suggests, "It was his conviction that, if men would adopt the Bible as the only standard of religious truth, and accept the meaning of words as determined simply by the rules of language, its true sense would be sufficiently obvious, and there would be universal agreement in relation to the things which it revealed" (*Memoirs, Book II*, 11). His counterpart, Barton Stone stated it this way: "We determine therefore to promote Christian union, to cast all such books to the moles and bats, and to take the Bible alone as the only standard of faith, practice and discipline" (Stone, *Christian Messenger,* Vol 2 269).

The biblical case was built on Paul's letter to young Timothy: "All scripture is inspired by God and is useful for teaching, for reproof, for correction, and for training in righteousness, so that everyone who belongs to God may be proficient, equipped for every good work" (II Timothy 3:16 – 17, NRSV). The combination of the "God-breathed word" and reasonable students drew Campbell and others to the assumption that logical and agreeable conclusions could and should be reached. A Campbell declared: "The Bible alone must always decide every question involving the nature, the character or the designs of the Christian institution. Outside of the apostolic canon, there is not, as it appears to me, one solid foot of terra firma on which to raise the superstructure ecclesiastic" (Richardson, *Memoirs, Book II,* 495). Scripture alone provided the truth; it was intelligible and self-explanatory as it unfolded into spiritual plans and specifications of the divine architect.

Consisting of the 66 individual writings of various genres, the 39 Old Testament and 27 New Testament books have been accepted by most Protestants as the canon of the Bible. These texts, selected from a number of writings, have been generally accepted as the "Bible" from the time of Luther and the Reformers. Written in three languages, passed down orally and/or copied by hand for many generations, the final translations into English are collected works of hundreds of scholars of all persuasions. A variety of translations provide options for English readers. A. Campbell offered his own translation.

In their zeal to understand this divine light, the early fathers became both speakers and writers; the writings provide us their understanding of what the narratives, poetry, history and letters meant. Though they agreed on many issues and compromised on others, they also agreed to disagree.

While avoiding the despised "creeds," their journals reflected different meanings in spite of T. Campbell's hope for reasoning and conclusions. Holding firmly to their view that the Bible was their sole guide, they pressed on, continuing to win people to their view of the truth of Jesus Christ as Lord of life.

In my formative years, I learned from my father who would probably be considered a "strict constructionist" seeking as literal an interpretation as possible. He taught that the Bible presented the inerrant word of God and that if one admitted to one problem it would open a flood gate to accepting other challenges and exceptions; ultimately, he believed that such an admission would destroy the Bible. Though not an absolute literalist or a legalist, he held this ground firmly as he taught. Accepting the idea that the Bible is our sole authority and only rule for faith and practice, his life was marked by simplicity and his preaching marked by careful exegesis of texts. Though cautious, he accepted others who did not accept his approach as brothers and sisters though he was unmovable.

When I arrived at Pacific Christian College, the general theme of our Bible faculty focused on "covenant theology." Though it differed from views taught in my seminary, it presented a refreshing way of understanding text even when not in complete agreement with some premises. Over the years, new faculty members have brought in different viewpoints. Not surprisingly, almost every view selected drew critics. Those who interpreted the Bible through a "premillennial" viewpoint found reasons to object to "amillennial" views. Others thought faculty views were "liberal" and demanded what they viewed as more "biblical" interpretations be taught. Thus, as Dr. North and others have suggested, the second premise of unity in the body has never been easy or comfortable. One does need advanced degrees in RM history to know that what began as a unity movement based on the authority of Scripture has proved extremely difficult to unify.

Ultimately, the two values still hold. Though not all will reach the same conclusion, "All scripture (the Bible) is inspired by God and is useful for teaching, for reproof, for correction, and for training in righteousness (our sole authority) so that everyone who belongs to God (all who profess that Jesus is the Christ, the Son of God, and their Savior) may be proficient, equipped for every good work" II Tim 3:16-17, NRSV). Must all agree that only the KJV is inspired and all other translations faulty? Must they agree that only a Restorationist view of the Bible is correct and that Calvinism, Premillennialism, and all other "isms" are flawed? Must all believe that all speak in tongues or that no one in our era has ever or will ever speak in tongues? Do all have to accept the view that Mary was a "perpetual" virgin? Or, for that matter, that it's not possible that she was? The power of this value – the Bible as our only rule of faith and practice – centers around the gift given by God in His son; and the single most complete account of that fact remains the book designated in our culture as the *Holy Bible*. We strive for unity; its importance centers in the book which holds John's Gospel, chapter 17: "I have given them your word . . . ." "Sanctify them in the truth, your word is truth." "I ask not only on behalf of these, but also on behalf of those who will believe in me through their word, that they may all be one. As you, Father, are in me and I am in you, may they also be in us, so that the world may believe that you have sent me."

Discussion Questions

1. Discuss Dr. North statement about the challenges of maintaining a harmonious spirit while differing on ways of viewing the Bible. Do you agree with his understanding that

holding to one's interpretation of Bible truth as the test of fellowship reduces the possibility of unifying a body of believers when others interpret texts differently?

2. Describing my father as a "strict constructionist" suggests that he believed in an infallible, inerrant view of the Bible and that suggested that even one error opened the door to a self-destructive path. He would find persons who hold an "open theology" viewpoint regarding God's "foreknowledge" disturbing while they might hold his as naïve; is it possible for persons holding such divergent viewpoints to remain a part of a historical movement? How can it happen?

3. If you had to select one of the two values as primary, which would you choose: a. the value of a unified body where compromises to one's personal views can be accepted or b. the value of biblical truth as a reasonable response for withholding fellowship from persons with whom there are disagreements? Where is (are) the line(s) to be drawn?

NOTES

NOTES

Lesson #3: Unity of Christians
David Lertis Matson

How big is your church? When asked that question, most Christians (especially preachers!) would probably respond by citing statistics—how many members they have on the roll or how many people attend worship on any given Sunday. But the question can take on a different meaning. Is your *vision* of the church big enough to include anyone who calls Jesus Lord, or do you draw the lines of fellowship more narrowly?

Perhaps the best known sentence in the writings of our Stone-Campbell heritage is the first proposition of Thomas Campbell's *Declaration and Address* of 1809: "The church of Christ upon earth is essentially, intentionally, and constitutionally one; consisting of all those in every place that profess their faith in Christ and obedience to Him in all things according to the Scriptures." On a nineteenth-century American frontier characterized by bitter and hostile divisions among Christians and denominations, this statement affirmed a striking but timeless truth: anyone who confesses Jesus as Lord and professes obedience to Him is part of the one universal church of Jesus Christ. So "big" would the church become in the thinking of the reformers Barton W. Stone and Alexander Campbell that they were willing to disagree on such important doctrines as the Trinity and substitutionary atonement (i.e., Jesus dying in our place for our sins). Nevertheless, they would still regard each other as brothers in Christ and members of the one church.

Much of our vision for Christian unity historically has taken its cue from Jesus' prayer for unity in the seventeenth chapter of the Gospel of John. In this prayer Jesus draws an ever-widening circle of fellowship as He prays for Himself (John 17:1-5), His immediate band of disciples (John 17:6-19), and all future believers (John 17:20-26). Rarely is the church of our own day addressed so directly on the pages of Scripture as it is in the third section of Jesus' prayer:

> I ask not only on behalf of these, but also on behalf of those who will believe in me through their word, that they may all be one. As you, Father, are in me and I am in you, may they also be in us, so that the world may believe that you have sent me (John 17:20-21, NRSV).

Jesus' prayer has as much to teach us about unity in our own day as it did in the day of Stone and the Campbells. First, Jesus affirms that unity is *vital* to our purpose. Our founders did not believe in unity for unity's sake. They believed in unity for the sake of mission and witness to the world. A divided church was by definition an ineffective church and a contradiction of its message of reconciliation. Jesus prays for the unity of His church precisely "so that the world may believe." Can a contentious, factious church have anything meaningful to say to a world torn by division and strife? Can a church at war effectively proclaim a gospel of peace? The answer is now a fashionable saying: The church must be *one* so that the world may be *won*.

Secondly, Jesus assumes that unity should be *visible* in our practice. It is no invisible unity for which Jesus prays. Unity must be concrete enough and demonstrable enough to

28

compel the world to believe. "By this everyone will know that you are my disciples, if you have love for one another" (John 13:35). In putting unity into practice, our founders did not opt for some doctrine of the "invisible church" that safely restricted unity only to certain "true" believers enrolled in heaven. Rather, they believed in the visible unity of all professed believers bearing their fruitful work on earth. As the *Declaration and Address* reminds us, it is the church of Christ upon earth that is essentially, intentionally and constitutionally one.

Thirdly, Jesus anticipates that unity will be **victorious** at his Parousia. Jesus goes on to pray: "The glory that you have given me I have given them, so that they may be one, as we are one" (John 17:22). The unity for which Jesus prays will be fully realized when we all come to share His glory in eternity. Our founders anticipated the day when the unity of God's people would usher in the glorious reign of the Messiah. The very title of Alexander Campbell's influential journal, *Millennial Harbinger*, which he published from 1830 until his death in 1866, gave expression to that great and blessed hope.

But how are Christians to achieve this unity? Our founders were clear: by restoring the church to its original intention as revealed in the New Testament. This effort to return to the church's foundational documents and first-century beliefs meant the rejection of any kind of creed or theological system as a basis for fellowship. If Christian unity was to be the means to evangelism, the restoration of historic "New Testament" Christianity was to be the means to Christian unity. Ironically, we have not always agreed on what that restoration means! But what is at least minimally clear from Jesus' prayer, is that the church is to be an inter-personal fellowship—"As you, Father, are *in* me and I am *in* you, may they also be *in* us" (emphasis mine). In our best theological thinking we have seen restoration not as copying a *pattern* but as participating in a *person* as branches organically related to the vine (John 15:1-11). As a notable statesman among us once put it, "restoration is ultimately a movement to restore the creation to the Creator."

Jesus believed in a really BIG church. Our founders did as well. Yet modern heirs of the Stone-Campbell Movement have not always lived up to this majestic vision. Sometimes we have limited our concept of the church to like-minded believers only.

Sometimes we have insisted on a particular definition of biblical faith and language. Sometimes we have made a stand on some controversial issue of our day a litmus test for Christian fellowship. Yet if we truly claim the oneness of the church, we must learn to find room for the "other sheep" who may not belong to our fold, that there may be "one flock, with one shepherd" (John 10:16). A poet has written:

> He drew a circle that shut me out—
> Rebel, heretic, thing to flout.
> But love and I had the wit to win—
> We drew a circle that took him in.

Are we drawing circles or drawing lines? How big is your church?

Discussion Questions

1. Have you ever experienced a church conflict or fight? What was the impact of that experience on you, your family and friends, and the surrounding community? Was the mission of your church adversely affected? How?

2. In your opinion are Christian denominations a good thing or a bad thing? Do they add to the diversity of the Body of Christ or are they inherently divisive? Explain.

3. Read Ephesians 4:1-16. What is the nature of Christian unity? In what sense do we already possess the unity of the Spirit (v. 3), while at the same time work to attain it (v. 13)?

4. In the Ephesians passage above, is there a conceptual difference between unity of the Spirit and unity of the faith? Is it possible to maintain the unity of the Spirit despite diversity of understanding? Does unity demand unity of knowledge?

5. What is more important to you and your church— truth or unity? Is dividing over "truth" actually an affront to the truth? Is the unity of the church part of the truth itself?

6. What are the "essentials" of the faith? What if Christians do not agree on what is essential? Is one person's "essentials" another person's "opinions"? How?

7. How might your church put Jesus' prayer into practice and demonstrate the visible unity of the church? Consider the following scenarios:

   a. A member of your church claims that he has been "baptized in the Spirit" and has recently begun speaking in tongues. While he has agreed not to be divisive on the issue, some members of your church have strongly suggested that he attend a different, more like-minded, church. Is this advice a practical solution to a potential problem, or is it making an unhealthy distinction among Christians?

b. Some members of your church believe very strongly that abortion is murder. Others believe that abortion, while not ideal, should be permitted under certain circumstances. The two factions threaten to split the church over the issue, each believing the other side is wrong and unchristian. What do you think should be done in this instance?

c. A special speaker comes to your church lecturing on the "evils of evolution." During the question-and-answer time, a member of your church, a high school biology teacher, points out the number of Christian scientists who think that evolution may be the way God chose to create the world. The speaker responds, "Well, then they're not *really* Christians if they believe that!" Is the speaker standing up for truth or compromising the unity of the church? Explain.

d. Members of your small group give political opinions with which you strongly disagree. In fact, you *can't stand* the candidate that they believe in so strongly. Can you still affirm them as fellow members of the Body of Christ? Can you do this wholeheartedly? Can you love them with Jesus' love? Explain.

NOTES

NOTES

Lesson #4: Covenant
Gene Sonnenberg

I once knew a man who justified his relationship with "the other woman" by appealing to the Old Covenant practice of polygamy (having two or more wives at the same time). "If God allowed a man to have more than one wife in Old Testament times," as his reasoning suggested, "then why would He not allow the same behavior in the church today?"

Many people confuse the practices and requirements in the Old Testament under the Old Covenant with what is allowed in the New. Likewise, blessings of the Old Covenant are being confused with the promises made to those under the New Covenant. Some Christians believe that 'keeping the Sabbath' is still a part of the New Covenant. Another example causing confusion today is related to worship. Today it is common for Christians to confuse Old Testament ideas of worship and what was practiced in the temple with the New Testament idea of worship primarily as service to our brothers and sisters in Christ and the larger world community. It is important to recognize the difference between the two covenants because our understanding of Scripture and ability to practically apply it depends upon such knowledge.

Both Alexander Campbell and his father, Thomas, came from the same religious background. It held that the Old

Covenant through Moses was still in some ways binding, in effect blurring the terms and promises of the two covenants. As a result, ideas and practices such as government under God became accepted in the New Covenant. Alexander's famous *Sermon on the Law* marked a radical departure from his tradition. He took the position of playing down the requirements of the Old Testament, and even today that position has been characteristic of most restoration churches. Campbell did not invent this understanding. It was bred out of fresh Bible study unhindered by tradition and encouraged by a quest for restoring the essentials as practiced by the earliest Christians. The early restoration leaders observed that mixing the terms of the Old and New Covenants creates legalism. To mix the predominantly physical promises of the Old Covenant, such as long life, prosperity and freedom of diseases, with the superior spiritual promises of the New Covenant gives rise to materialism and a prosperity gospel. Common examples today include the thinking of some Christians that financial prosperity or freedom from illness are indicators of a superior "walk" in the Lord. We know from Jesus' own teachings that it was not His plan to establish an earthly kingdom of wealth and palaces; rather, He showed how the kingdom was already among them.

People have been contract makers from the beginning of civilization. The legal codes of ancient peoples testify to this practice of making contracts or covenants. The usual form included naming the parties involved, the terms required and the promises for keeping or breaking the agreement. Covenants were for the benefit of both parties.

It was natural for God to use this common format when establishing a relationship with humankind. To break the agreement meant that the benefits ceased and the penalties followed. God entered into a special covenant with Abram intending that through him all the nations of the world would be blessed. God also entered into a contract with the people of

Israel through Moses for the creation of a people through whom a deliverer would come. The Messiah would be the means by which the nations of the world would be blessed. The Old Covenant through Moses included the familiar components of a covenant. God and the people of Israel were involved as the parties. The 613 laws for Israel were the terms. The promises were the mutual benefits or curses which followed as consequences for keeping or not keeping the contract. God would receive a people through whom He could work; and Israel would receive the land of Canaan, long life, freedom from disease, prosperity, many descendents and victory in battle.

God announced that He would make a new covenant (Jeremiah 31:30-33). He would remove the old agreement set down in stone (Ten Commandments) and write it on the human heart, giving to each person who entered into the New Covenant a new Spirit. Israel looked forward to this New Covenant but mistakenly believed that it would be their blessing and their exclusive responsibility to maintain. God's plan, however, was that all humanity would be included equally with the same terms and the same blessings. There was to be no favored nation status for Israel nor anyone else for ". . . God does not show favoritism" (Romans 2:11). God was sending a new Moses (Jesus), creating a New Covenant, fulfilling the old law and replacing it with a new law of love (hesed). God was leading all humankind through a new exodus (out of sin), creating a new Israel (the church) and leading them into a new land of promise (the abundant life through Jesus).

In this New Covenant baptism became the oath of covenant entry, and the Lord's Supper a weekly covenant renewal ceremony. No longer were the covenant terms the keeping of a legal code; rather, the new terms became commitment to growing in Christlikeness and participation in the mission of the church. The prominent feature of living this new life is the new standard of love for even one's enemies. Love is a fulfillment of the entire Old Testament legal code (Romans 13:8-14).

The Campbell's held an understanding of the New Covenant faith that led them to reject whatever was not made essential by Jesus and those whom He taught. For many Christians today the problem with which they wrestle is that of how to resolve the tension between the Old Testament and the New Testament. The early church saw the problem differently. For them the problem was how to reconcile the Old Covenant Scriptures with Jesus himself. The New Testament Scriptures are the solution. These "New" Scriptures demonstrate how the early church was taught to filter the Old Covenant Scripture through the teaching of Jesus, their new "Moses." We, too, need to view the Old Covenant through the lens of Jesus and His teachings.

Covenant is not some sterile idea. Rather, it speaks of an interactive adventure with a gracious relational God. The idea of covenant therefore, is a primary biblical idea for understanding God's working with humankind in the present, as well as the past. God still relates to us in covenantal terms. He has offered salvation to all people (parties). The terms are the same for all; trusting in Jesus as our new Lord and acting in His best interest in thankful response to His gift of salvation. The new promises are superior to all offered previously—forgiveness, eternal life, the gift of the Holy Spirit as Helper, fellowship with all in the community of God, and even the promise of suffering with and on behalf of Christ. That is the New Covenant into which we have entered. It is ratified in the blood of Christ and guaranteed by the seal of God's own Spirit in every child of God. It is the way God has chosen to create a new humanity and restore His family to Himself.

Discussion Questions

1. Why is it important to understand the difference between the Old and New Covenants? How do the terms covenant and hesed translate in the New Testament?

2. How do the New and Old Covenants compare? Discuss the differences.

Covenant?	OLD	NEW
Parties	God and Israel	God and all the nations
Terms	613 Laws	Christlikeness and the Great Commission
Promises	Physical: Land, Material Prosperity, Long Life, Victory in Battle, Many Children, Freedom from disease.	Eternal Life, Forgiveness, Holy Spirit indwelling each Believer, Community with all God's People, Suffering for Christ

3. In what ways is the New Covenant superior to the Old? (Hebrews chapters 3-12) What difference does this make in your life?

a. Jesus is superior as High Priest and to Moses

b. Jesus offers superior priesthood, sacrifice and rewards

4. Is the Christian today still under the "ten commandments"? Why or why not?

5. Is Jesus more interested in the letter of the law or the heart? Explain.

6. In what ways are Christians today at risk of practicing legalism? Is there no room for the legalistic thinker?

7. How can the covenant of marriage be used as an example to illustrate Old and New Covenant differences? See Ephesians 5:21-33.

     a. Entering the covenant

     b. Keeping the covenant

     c. Breeching the covenant

8. How does God's action in Christ provoke and encourage me to want to demonstrate gratitude to God for the good He has done for me? How do you apply hesed here?

9. *Optional Advanced Question*: The Restoration Movement has contributed to the church in many ways. Cite other examples.

     a. Focus on baptism and Lord's Supper

     b. Legalism

     c. New Covenant practices

NOTES

NOTES

Lesson #5: Mission and World Evangelism
Kevin "Kip" Lines

After the worship service, the chorus of the Turkana song echoed in my mind, *"Nyali erot lo?"* (Which pathway is this that we are on?) *"Erot a Yesu."* (This is the path of Jesus.) *"Elipa ekapolon!"* (Pray to the Lord for guidance!) As missionaries serving in the remote NW corner of Kenya among the Turkana people from 1999-2008, my wife Katy and I often reflected on that question, "Which pathway is this we are on?"

Sometimes the question arose when we were lost following some dirt track on the way to another village, but often it arose in reflection on our lives as missionaries. How in the world did we journey from Pennsylvania (myself) and Colorado (Katy) to this place in the middle of Africa? Who were *we* to bring this message from God to the people of Turkana? What was this crazy path we were on? The answer came to us in this simple Turkana chorus, "this is the path of Jesus!" When we are willing to follow in the path of Jesus, willing to serve as he served, to pray the things that he prayed for, and to love as he loved… there's no telling where that path might lead. It might even lead to the ends of the earth!

Both of our paths began in the local church, specifically in Restoration Movement (RM) churches.

Growing up in a Christian Church in Pennsylvania, I was raised with a sense that both supporting missions and actively engaging in evangelism were activities in which all Christians were expected to participate through the church. I remember missionaries that our church supported visiting from Ghana, Hawaii and Zimbabwe. They always had the best stories, I thought, although the slide shows seemed a bit too long! As a high school student, I attended an 8-week course on "lifestyle evangelism" at my church, and was convinced at an early age that if the Good News really was good, it was something that needed to be shared with others. I wanted to be part of that ministry of reconciliation.

It wasn't until college that I began to understand the distinctiveness of the RM's commitment to mission and evangelism. While I learned that one of the most important ideals of the Movement was the unity of the Church (see lesson #3), I later realized that unity was not an end in itself, but was meant to lead into more effective evangelism. Writing in 1824, Alexander Campbell made clear his concern that, without unity among Christians, our efforts in "conversion of the world" would be in vain (*Christian Baptist*, 2:135, 1824). He was convinced that division among Christians would be the greatest stumbling block to non-Christians accepting Jesus as Lord (*Christian Baptist*, 1:40-42, 1824). Our unity as Christians within individual congregations, without sectarian and denominational divisions, could be a key strategy in our evangelistic mission. This affirms Jesus' earnest prayer for the Church in John 17; not merely for a unity in the Church so we could all coexist, but "so that the world may believe" (John 17:21).

This mission begins in the local church. Following the model of Paul and Barnabas being sent out from the congregation at Antioch (Acts 13), RM churches were early leaders in the modern Protestant missionary movement in America. As congregations were sending out missionaries, some churches gathered to form a cooperative mission sending organization in 1849, the Foreign Christian Missionary Society, in which more than 100 representatives from 100 RM churches worked together to send a missionary to Jerusalem. The RM churches were also leaders in the formation of the Christian Women's Board of Missions, during an era when women missionaries outnumbered male missionaries almost 2:1. These mission boards were never seen as a replacement for the role of the local church, but as cooperative organizations to help churches do even more in their mission efforts.

As expected from a Christian unity movement, representatives from both of these RM mission boards were present at the influential 1910 World Missionary Conference in Edinburgh, Scotland, including a 12 year old boy named Donald McGavran. McGavran attended with his parents, and would later serve as a 3rd generation RM missionary in India. McGavran went on to become one of the leading missiologists of the 20th century, utilizing application of the social sciences for mission and founding a graduate theological school devoted to church growth and evangelism at Northwest Christian College. McGavran's School of Church Growth outgrew NCC and moved to Fuller Theological Seminary, where missionaries and church planters from all over the world still study today.

By the 1960s, most of the RM mission sending organizations that began in the Christian Churches were highly influenced by this Church Growth/Church Planting model of missions, with many sending their missionaries for at least one year of graduate education at Fuller before serving on the mission field. Missionaries were trained to use the best of cultural anthropology and linguistics to better understand and contextualize the message of the Gospel as they incarnated God's love in local languages, living among people in vulnerability, in the model of Jesus' incarnation.

Our Movement's reliance on the authority of Scripture as a core value helps us understand why participating in God's mission through missions and evangelism has been, and continues to be, part of our identity. The entire story of the Old and New Testaments is the story of God's mission, a metanarrative of God's relationship with God's people and His desire for all people to be included in the story. We understand that as the Church, we are people engaged in God's mission; we are a missional people.

Through faith in Jesus we are heirs of the blessings and promises of the covenant with Abraham (Gen 12:2-3). But we are not a blessed, chosen people, a royal priesthood, merely for our own benefit (1 Pet 2:29). We have received these blessings so that we can continue in God's blessing of all the nations, all the people of the earth through His people. Our God is not limited solely to us. God is not our God alone, but the God of the universe, the God of *all* people. While God's love and desire to be in relationship with all people is universal, we have received a specific revelation directly from God through the person of Jesus; that because of Jesus' birth, life, death and resurrection, the Good News of the Kingdom of God is even more clearly a message for *all* people.

Following the Protestant Reformation, more than 200 years passed before the Church began to re-envision mission, to restore the idea that the Church is still a part of God's mission today. For hundreds of years, Mathew 28:16-20 was interpreted as applying only to the original followers of Jesus. Thankfully, we have come to understand again that Jesus is also telling *us* to "go!" Telling *us* tocross borders and boundaries in our increasingly culturally diverse neighborhoods. Telling *us* to continue to raise up and send out missionaries.

New challenges and opportunities have opened up to us today in mission and world evangelism. One major shift is that mission is no longer one directional. There are no longer simply missionary senders and receivers. We are now living in a time when churches around the world are sending their own missionaries, sometimes without the support of the Western church and sometimes in partnership. This is great news, but does it mean that our job is finished? No!

Increasingly, urban centers in Europe and North America have become post-Christian, places where people have grown-up completely outside the context of the church. In a complex, globalized world we need to be more creative in our mission and evangelism efforts. Answering the question of what it means for people in cities (quickly approaching 60% of the world's population) to understand the message of Jesus as Good News will require a new generation of creative missionaries. We need missionaries sent out by their churches, no longer simply to nation states or to people groups, but to migrants and transnationals; people who move and live in one place but identify with another. We need a new wave of missionaries who can negotiate postmodern ambiguity and interact with those of other major world religions with humility, love and authenticity in regard to the Lordship of Jesus. We need missionaries who do not divide their ministries into either "preaching" or "social action," but view both as part of a holistic approach.

As the world increases in complexity, the ideals of the Restoration Movement will continue to serve us well: a foundation in the Scriptures, a focus on the local church's participation in God's mission, and seeking unity with all Christians under the Lordship of Jesus. We never know where we might end up! The churches in Kenya, planted by CMF International among the Turkana and the Maasai are now officially called the Community Christian Church. No longer relying on American missionaries for guidance and support, the Community Christian Churches in Kenya have recently formed their own missionary sending agency. They plan to work together to send Kenyan missionaries to the least reached areas of Kenya, Tanzania and even South Sudan. Perhaps a Kenyan missionary will even be sent to work alongside your church in an urban center in America. And then she and her husband will look around and ask themselves, "Which path are we on?" This is the path of Jesus!

Discussion Questions:

1. A member of your church feels called to pursue full-time intercultural mission work as a career. Your church has never had a missionary sent out from within your congregation. What should be done?

2. Some members of your church are convinced that some people, especially those far away who live very differently than we do, are better off if they have never heard of Christ, so they should just be left alone. How do you respond to this way of thinking?

3. We are not alone anymore. Few people in the world live in communities where there is one ethnic and cultural group in isolation. This presents a new challenge to the church. No longer is mission work, as it was traditionally thought of, a task only for missionaries in far-off lands. Today we find ourselves in diverse and multicultural communities. How do you feel about diversity in the church? When you look around your church community is it representative of the diverse community you live in? Why or why not?

4. God desires a reconciled relationship with all people. The challenge to make disciples is clear. In making disciples, we are called to share the gospel in a manner that can be understood by those hearing. How can you avoid straying from Scriptural teachings into cultural teachings while still making the gospel message understandable in a diverse setting?

5. People can be very uncomfortable with differences, especially in worship styles. As we reach out to the world for Christ, sharing God's Good News and the salvation provided through Jesus Christ, what should the worship services look like in other areas of the world that are different form your own? What are the essentials of worship and what can be left up to culturally diverse ways of approaching worship of God?

6. What are you willing to do, to give up, to pray for and to seek out in order to pursue God's mission of reconciling with all people? Is the evangelization of the world your responsibility or someone else's responsibility? Why? How can we encourage each other to identify and respond to their own unique callings?

NOTES

NOTES

NOTES

Lesson #6: The Priesthood of All Believers
Philip Towne

When one pictures a priest in his or her mind, what is the first image that might arise? For those from a Roman Catholic background, the image of the leader of their local congregation, one who hears confession and administers the sacraments might come to mind. Others imagine a highly decorated image like that described in the Old Testament. Some see a pagan performing a ritual dance, chanting to an unknown tongue.

While the protestant church has never had the office of priest as part of its structure, it has nevertheless has established clerical leaders that have nearly functioned as such. The Protestant Reformation led the church away from such an office officially and emphasized the priesthood of all believers, the priestly mediators removed from the equation. However, for many churches, a structure remains that have some sort of mediator within them. Instead of a priestly mediator, many pastors and bishops have functioned as a priestly figure.

The Roman Catholic view of the church tends to be very sacramental in its focus. The church is the people of God in the world, but only after they have entered into the church through proper sacraments, primarily baptism and communion. Previously, the church held the perspective that there was no salvation for individuals outside of the Roman Catholic Church. However, in recent years this point was expanded to include other church groups that are able to fall under the universal church. Although recently broadened, there remains a very highly organized and hierarchical structure that is the church, in which the priest is the primary mediator between God and people.

Protestant reformer Martin Luther believed the church is made up of a priesthood of all believers, which to him, went in direct contradiction to the Catholic perspective. While specific offices and positions in the church were allowable to him, he detested the hierarchical nature of the Roman Catholic Church. He believed instead that the church was to be a place where the gospel is preached and the sacraments are administered by and for all people. He did not believe the sacraments provided an entrance into the church, as the Catholic perspective maintained, but rather the church was the body of people amongst which this happens. The purpose of the church then is to preach the gospel through word and sacrament, as well as serving one another, while empowering more than just the priests to do so (see 1 Peter 2:9).

Although the structure of the church as a whole is not the problem, it can at times get in the way of the idea of the priesthood of all believers. While accepting specific positions or offices within the church, we must cautiously make these secondary to the fellowship of believers. In fact, structure and expertise are both needed to avoid chaos and confusion within the church. However, often times an overemphasis on structure and institutionalization have negatively affected the effective service of the church. The church structure itself should be focused around the preparing of believers to do the work of ministry and for building up of the body of Christ (Ephesians 4:11-13).

Amongst Restoration Movement (RM) churches this notion of the priesthood of all believers has been extended and emphasized as a key value. The movement to embrace not just ordained clergy, but all believers continues and does not just give all people access to be ministers of the gospel, but instead extends to all believers in fact being responsible to be ministers. No longer is a human mediator needed, but rather Christ himself functions as the sole mediator (1 Tim. 2:5). While each person may help a brother or sister move closer to Christ, there is no necessary mediator of a priest to do so. Within the RM tradition, the elimination of the clergy/laity distinction allows all to play a part in ministry. This is visible in part through the serving of the Lord's Supper, which all believers have ability to do without special conditions.

If the church is the people of God, then it follows naturally that those under the new covenant set forth by Jesus no longer need a priestly mediator other than Christ himself. Christ, the great high priest, alone deserves our service (Hebrews 4:14; I Peter 2:9). All members of the church are the people of God. Therefore, they are responsible for other people, because the Church itself is the mediator between God and the world, obligated to pray for the world, devote themselves to service of others, and as witnesses of God's work in the world.

The priesthood of all believers is a fellowship in which all Christians, instead of living for themselves, live before God for others and are, in turn, supported by others. Deitrich Bonhoeffer wrote, "The church is church only when it is there for others."[1] Bonhoeffer's emphasis on living for the sake of others in the world strikes a chord.

---

[1] Bonhoeffer, Dietrich, Letters and Papers from Prison (Minneapolis, MN: Fortress, 2010), 503.

Often times, the church is thought of as a special organization, containing elect believers separated from the world. Bonhoeffer's idea of being "for" the world envisions the church as a place that desires good and loves the world. Our jobs as "priests" in the world demand that we mediate the love and grace of Jesus to all around us.

Imagine what the church could look like if we all took seriously this idea of the priesthood of all believers. Imagine the way we might perceive ministry differently than we sometimes do. Rather than waiting for "the" pastor or priest to perform his or her duty, we would instead take the initiative to do what God has called us to, that is for us each to be a participant in the mission of God in the world. No longer are we under the understanding that a priestly mediator stands between us and God. Rather, each has become a priest, mediating the good news of Jesus to the world. We each serve in our vocations, all called to ministry. None possess a higher calling than others. While our roles look quite different, we all work as one in the body of Christ.

"There are different kinds of gifts, but the same Spirit distributes them. There are different kinds of service, but the same Lord. There are different kinds of working, but in all of them and in everyone it is the same God at work" (1 Cor. 12:4-6).

Discussion Questions:

1. What image does the word "priest" bring to your mind? Why?

2. Look up the verses Revelation 1:4-6 and 1 Peter 2:9. Both talk about believers being a priesthood. What do you imagine this to look like?

3. As part of the priesthood of all believers, we are each called into ministry, whether we have a church related job or not. What do you feel is your job as part of this priesthood?

4. When you think of the church you attend or one you have attended, do you think this idea of all people being ministers or priests has been embraced?

5. Read Ephesians 4:11-13. How do you see these verses fitting with the idea of the priesthood of all believers?

6. What role does the local church congregation serve if all are ministers or priests?

7. If we take seriously the idea of the priesthood of all believers, does this change anything about the way we currently live? Does this change how we relate to what we call "church"?

NOTES

NOTES

NOTES

Lesson #7: Servant Leadership
Joe Grana

There is a group of pilgrims belonging to a religious order on a spiritual journey in search of wisdom and "themselves." Leo, one of their companions, is their servant. Leo takes care of all the daily chores: cooking, cleaning and packing for the journey. In the evening he encourages the pilgrims by singing, telling stories and creating a joyful atmosphere.

Mysteriously, Leo disappears one morning. No one seems to know where he has gone. He is greatly missed because now no one cooks breakfast; no one packs and no one sings. The joyful atmosphere is gone and the companions are lost without Leo. The travelers start to turn on each other. They do not find the wisdom they are looking for; in fact, their spiritual journey ends abruptly.

Years later, one of the members finds Leo and meets again with the order that sponsored the journey. Much to his surprise he discovers that Leo, in fact, is head of the order. He is the "guiding spirit, a great and noble leader." (Greenleaf, p. 7) Leo's leadership, however, is the result of being a servant first.

Robert Greenleaf of AT&T related this story in his book: *Servant Leadership* (1977). Upon reflection of Leo's example and what servant leadership is, Greenleaf came up with these applications:

1. Servant leaders respond to problems and conflict by listening first (p. 17).
2. Servant leaders accept the person and evaluate performance (pp. 20, 21).
3. Servant leaders have a broadened sense of awareness (pp. 27, 28).
4. Servant leaders persuade one person at a time (p. 29).

Alexander Campbell did not stress the term servant leader. Instead, he stressed being a disciple of Christ. Yet, the Restoration Movement values this position. Jesus is the leader of a great "religious order." However, He demonstrated His leadership by "taking the very nature of a servant" (Philippians 2:7). As all Christians are disciples, so all Christians are to be servants: just like Leo, just like Jesus!

Servant and leader are terms that seem to be opposites. Certainly, that view is true in society as a whole. However, a shift has been occurring for some time in the corporate world. The concept of leaders serving their followers has caught on in some companies. Robert Greenleaf writes:

> The servant-leader is a servant first…. It begins with the natural feeling that one wants to serve, to serve first. The conscious choice brings one to aspire to lead…the difference manifests itself in the care taken by the servant – first to make sure that other people's highest priority needs are being served. The best test, and difficult to administer, is: do those served grow as persons; do they, while being served, become healthier, wiser, freer, more autonomous, more likely themselves to become servants? And what is the effect on the least privileged in society; will they

benefit, or at least, not be further deprived? (pp.13, 14)

Of course the church has long known this idea. Jesus said, "...the son of man came not to be served, but to serve, and to give his life as a ransom for many" (Matthew 20:28). Again, Jesus stated, "The greatest among you will be your servant. For whoever exalts himself will be humbled and whoever humbles himself will be exalted" (Matthew 23:11-12).

In John 13:1-12 we read about Jesus washing the feet of the apostles. Jesus is the creator of the universe. Jesus is the most powerful person ever. Jesus is God! Yet... he chooses to wash the dirty feet of weak men. Men who sin. Men who get confused! Men who want to lead and rule, but do not understand how. Jesus shows them how. God leads by serving! A servant is what He is, deep down inside! .

Many other texts stress this concept that Jesus lived out: Luke 22:26, 27; John 12:20-26; I Peter 4:10, 11; Mark 9:33-37; and II Corinthians 6:1-10. Select some of these verses and reflect upon them.

The point of understanding this concept is one of perspective. In a world of "dog eat dog" and "look out for number one," servant Leadership makes little sense. Where power is viewed as having limits, one will not desire to let go of any of it. But, from God's perspective, as one who was willing to humble Himself and become man and then to die on a cross, it makes all the sense in the universe!

The terms minister and deacon come from a Greek word meaning servant. People in the office of minister or deacon are to express their position by serving the people for whom they are responsible.

Hope International University has a simple, but profound slogan which encapsulates the servant leadership concept: "Where Learning Leads to Serving." Unfortunately, as we readily observe in a fallen world, learning can lead to all kinds of deviant behavior. People can just become smarter in how to do evil. Identity theft is a prime example. Somehow someone on the east coast reproduced my credit card and used it in six stores, charging $1,200 in merchandise in one day! That person used their learning to deceive and defraud.

However, when the goal is serving, learning can lead to all kinds of beneficial behavior. People in the helping professions use their learning to benefit others. Even the Internet, television, video, etc. can be used to serve people's needs. These tools, designed by people of great learning, can be used to serve the world if in the hands of people with pure motives.

At Hope International University our learning leads to a goal of serving the world. Educated Christians have the potential to be servant leaders who impact the world for Christ! May the church today model servant leadership. May the corporate world discover the wisdom of this principle as Christians live it out in the real world!

Discussion Questions:

1. How do you define servant? Define leader?

2. How do you reconcile the paradox of a leader who serves?

3. How realistic is it in your world to be a servant leader?

4. How is this concept lived out in your church?

5. In what ways do you demonstrate servant leadership? How could you grow in this area?

6. In your opinion, what historical figures were servant leaders? What was their impact? Why?

7. Name someone you know who is a servant leader. Explain.

8. Analyze and describe how Jesus lived this concept.

9. What makes people hesitate to believe and live by this concept?

NOTES

NOTES

NOTES

Lesson # 8: The Church
K.C. Richardson

"Can a person be a Christian without the church?" Many today would answer "yes" to that frequently asked question. Some people see no use for the church when they can be "spiritual" on their own time and in their own ways. For others, the church's ancient truths seem irrelevant to the questions troubling our modern world. Still others claim that the church actually hinders true discipleship with its hypocrisy and petty doctrinal disputes.

We might assume that these pessimistic views of the church are a byproduct of our postmodern 21st century American society. We live in a time when many traditional institutions are viewed with skepticism about their continuing value in a changing world. Yet, such doubts are not really new. In the early 19th century, many Americans, including several of the "founding fathers," were concerned about the church's place in American society. Private faith, they agreed, would be beneficial to the new republic, but the history of violent wars carried out in the name of religion provided ample evidence to them that a powerful institutional church posed a threat to liberty and peace. The church was a problem to be managed rather than a solution to be celebrated.

The early leaders of the Stone-Campbell Movement shared some of these concerns. They too not only witnessed, but in many cases had personally experienced, the pain caused by a divided church. The difference, however, was that for these early leaders the church was not a failed institution to be abandoned but a viable organism in need of reform. In fact, they frequently described their efforts in this way, not as a "restoration" of the authentic church, as if it had been lost from history for 1800 years, but as a continuing "reformation." They realized that the church is nothing less than the body of Christ ordained by God to carry out his purpose and must therefore be loved and served. For this reason, the church has always been at the very heart of the theological reflection of the Stone-Campbell Movement.

Throughout the New Testament, the church is described as a "fellowship" (*koinōnia*). This idea of *koinōnia* suggests three important themes which have traditionally been emphasized by Stone-Campbell churches.

1. The Church is One

Authentic Christian *koinōnia* requires unity among Christians, a quest that was one of the hallmarks of the early Stone-Campbell Movement. In the *Declaration and Address*, commonly recognized as one of the movement's founding documents, Thomas Campbell wrote that "the church upon earthy is essentially, intentionally, and constitutionally one." This statement may have surprised many in the early 19th century who observed its fractured state, but Campbell's point was that the church is one, even when Christians fail to recognize this fact and act accordingly. It is one because it belongs to God, not to its human participants. The plea of Stone-Campbell churches has been that Christians not only recognize the oneness of the church but also actively seek ways to bear witness to this God-given unity.

Unity in the midst of diversity is a worthy human aspiration which finds expression in many contemporary institutions. Yet an essential feature of Christian unity, which makes it unique and more durable than the fellowship enjoyed in other human organizations, is that it originates in the cross. Christians enjoy the gift of being reconciled to one another because they have been "restored" to a relationship with God through the atoning sacrifice of Christ. Speaking of the strained relations between Jews and Gentiles, Paul writes in Ephesians 2 of the human reconciliation that only the cross can accomplish, "He has abolished the law with its commandments and ordinances, *that he might create in himself one new humanity in place of the two, thus making peace, and might reconcile both groups to God in one body, through the cross, thus putting to death the hostility through it*" (15-16, emphasis added). Churches of the Stone-Campbell Movement have traditionally borne witness to the idea that Christian unity is not simply the result of human goodwill but rather a gift of God made possible through Christ.

2. The Church is Universal

A second important theme is that while Christian *koinōnia* is experienced first and foremost in the local congregation, the global and historical implications of *koinōnia* must also be recognized. Churches of the Stone-Campbell heritage have frequently affirmed the "catholicity" of the church by highlighting the universally observed elements of Christian faith and practice, rather than local and peculiar ones. For example, a biblical confession like, "Jesus Christ is Lord" has been preferred to more lengthy creeds because all Christians can affirm this simple statement. Likewise, Stone-Campbell churches practice baptism and the Lord's Supper because they recognize these to be ancient ordinances established by Christ and observed by the earliest Christians. When local assemblies embrace these ancient expressions of faith and practice, they affirm their connection with the historic and universal church.

For most of their history, churches of the Stone-Campbell tradition adopted a "congregational" form of organization with the understanding that the church is embodied in the local Christian assembly, not in a larger denominational structure. One advantage of this system is the freedom it provides. Acting simply under the authority of Christ, local congregations are free to engage in reform and promote Christian unity without the need for denominational approval. A congregational structure also allows for the expression of diversity, whether it be in the style of worship or in doctrinal matters. The familiar slogan: "in essentials unity, in non-essentials liberty, and in all things love" expresses well the value placed upon Christian freedom.

A potential danger of this freedom, however, is that it may lead to insularity and sectarianism, a danger that has in fact manifested itself at various times in Stone-Campbell history. Instead of affirming the slogan, "We are not the only Christians, but Christians only," a congregational structure could communicate "we *are* the only Christians." But this is to misunderstand the relationship between the local and universal expressions of the church. Once again in the *Declaration and Address*, Campbell stated that "although the church of Christ upon earth must necessarily exist in particular and distinct societies, locally separate from one another...there ought to be no schisms, no uncharitable divisions among them." In other words, even though Christians experience church in particular local assemblies, this should not be the result of, nor should it imply, division among them.

3. The Church has a Mission

Stone-Campbell churches have also affirmed a third truth which is suggested by the concept of *koinōnia*: the church is a serving community with a mission. In secular usage in the New Testament era, *koinōnia* sometimes described a contractual relationship, for example an agreement between business partners. This use of the term suggests working together toward a common goal or purpose. A similar idea can be seen in the Stone-Campbell tradition. As worthy a goal as it might be to create an inclusive, loving, and mutually supportive community for its own sake, the primary reason for pursuing Christian unity was to enable the church to be more effective in its mission. Frequently cited is Jesus' prayer in John 17 in which he asks for the unity of his disciples, "so that the world might believe" (17:21). Jesus recognized that the church's witness to the gospel is only as effective as the extent of its unity.

Perhaps this final theme is the best response to the question, "Does the Christian really need the church?" It is in the church that the Christian finds a community in which to discover, embrace, and carry out his or her God-given vocation. In the church there should be no passive observers; everyone has an integral role to play as the church seeks to fulfill its Great Commission of going into all the world to make disciples (Matthew 28:19). Paul understood the church to be the body of Christ and made the point that every member of the body has an essential function, even those who appear too humble and insignificant by worldly standards (1 Corinthians 12:12-31). The church is also a "priesthood of all believers" (1 Peter 2:5). This means that even though Stone-Campbell churches do practice ordination and support their ministers financially, they have been reluctant to make a clear distinction between clergy and laity, the "religious professionals" and the "people in the pew." All Christians are considered to be ordained for ministry by virtue of their baptism at which they enter the New Covenant and accept not only its blessings but also the calling to Christian service that goes with it.

Even though the institutional church seems to have fallen on difficult times in recent years and we frequently hear predictions of its demise, it remains the body of Christ beloved by God and therefore inherently valuable. This is not to say that the church is without blemishes and flaws. Christians must be honest about these and commit themselves to the difficult work of ongoing reformation for the sake of the church's witness. To value the church enough to be committed to this continuing reformation is a worthy goal for those who claim the Stone-Campbell heritage.

Discussion Questions:

1. Do you agree that there has been a decline in the perceived value of the church in our society today? What are some reasons for this?

2. What are some alternative venues for experiencing fellowship in our contemporary world other than the church? What does the church offer that these other options do not? How would you respond to someone who says, "I don't really need the church; I can experience 'community' elsewhere"?

3. How would you define Christian unity? What are some ways in which your church promotes Christian unity?

4. How can Christian unity be achieved in a non-denominational or "congregational" form of church organization? If we worship in separate, local, and diverse congregations that do not agree on a variety of issues, doesn't that mean the church is divided?

5. In what ways have you experienced the concept of the "priesthood of all believers"? How has your church

helped you discover and develop your gifts for service? How do you see your role in the body of Christ as a participant in the church's mission?

NOTES

NOTES

NOTES

Lesson #9: Freedom of Interpretation
William R. Baker

The most cherished of all American values is freedom. Freedom of expression, freedom of religion, freedom of lifestyle choice, freedom of movement, and more, are all integral aspects of our lives. Freedom is what people from most other countries crave when they speak of the desire to come to America.

But freedom is also an integral plank in the heritage of the Stone-Campbell Movement. Our religious heritage could only have bubbled up from the freedom already planted in the soil of American culture by our founding fathers. Like Thomas Jefferson and others, Barton W. Stone, Alexander Campbell, and his father Thomas Campbell were heavily influenced by the writings of John Locke. In his 1689 Letter Concerning Toleration, Locke wrote: "I esteem that toleration to be the chief characteristic of the true Church." He goes on: "However clearly we may think this or the other doctrines to be deduced from Scripture, we ought not therefore impose it upon others as a necessary article of faith, because we believe it to be rule of faith." These principles of freedom of interpretation found their way into one of the founding documents of the Stone-Campbell Movement.

In less than two years after his arrival from Scotland and settling in Western Pennsylvania in 1807, Thomas Campbell penned what is considered the charter document of the Stone-Campbell Movement. This 90-page document, called the *Declaration and Address of the Christian Association of Washington*, would fuel the life-long efforts of his son, Alexander, who would turn its ideals into a new church movement. Within these pages are the ideals, principles, and a plan for forging true and unified Christianity in this new land brimming with opportunity, no longer tied to the barriers to unity constructed by the bickering of Christianity in Europe. Foundational to the *Declaration and Address* is the principle of freedom of interpretation.

Freedom of religion is based on the respect and dignity all people deserve as an "inalienable right." Freedom of interpretation draws on this same principle. Regardless of how central a truth or how marginal a truth from Scripture might be, how can anyone be held accountable to assent to it unless she is convinced it is true? Campbell wants to protect the right to private judgment regarding scriptural interpretation along with the idea that many truths of Scripture are clear, or as he says "express." His concern is also that Christians think for themselves and not automatically sign off on lists of theological statements that are required for membership in certain denominations.

Within Campbell's document are thirteen propositions that synthesis his thinking. Two of these, proposition six and seven, focus on freedom of interpretation. Proposition Six recognizes that interpretation of Scripture leads to a variety of "doctrines and inferences" that are evident enough for all believers (the church) to confess wholeheartedly as true. However, most such deductions and inferences may be evident only to a certain band of believers or even to a lone individual. Regarding the latter, Campbell concludes: "No such deductions or inferential truths out to have any place in the Church's confession." The Church's confession ought to be what Christians universally hold to be true and be a point of unity rather than division.

Proposition Seven expands on the issue of deductions and inference. It re-emphasizes their divisive tendency. But it also observes how crucial it is for the church, and interpreters on its behalf, to be free to continue to investigate the richness of Scripture for its truths.These truths, even inferred, may be held by individuals or groups. Plus, they should have freedom to convince others and even the Church as whole to believe them to be faithful truth from Scripture. As Christians we should also be growing in what we understand from Scripture. And so, both believers and the church can and should continue to mature in this way.

The point, though, is that both you and I have the freedom to hold to our beliefs--even if others are not convinced. However, we don't have the right to demand others agree with us and then write them of as not really being Christians if they don't. Campbell's principles boil down to this practical solution: we agree to disagree and we agree to agree. It is a matter of honor and respect as brothers and sisters in Christ. The principle holds for relationships between denominations and local churches as well.

Thomas Campbell believes this is one of the key solutions to unite the church. In this way the church, which is already "one in Christ" can function as one. It's not surprising that Alexander Campbell would later to assert the motto that we should have "no creed but Christ." We as the universal church can surely agree to that. And we can agree on more than that. But the principle is that many things have to be discussable because many things are not as obvious as sometimes people think they are. In his long Appendix to his *Declaration* Thomas Campbell even asserts that complete unity on the meaning of Scripture is "morally impossible, all the things considered." He cannot "conceive what desirable purpose such unity of sentiment would serve" because it would eliminate development of the virtue of "forbearance' that Christians need to develop in order to learn from one another.

Thomas Campbell's *Declaration and Address* is a remarkable achievement for its day that continues to have relevance for the life of the church, for congregations, and for individual believers. Its internal logic may be summarized as follows:

1) Scripture contains truth that can be recognized universally by all believers.

2) Scripture contains truth that is not recognized universally by all believers.

3) Believers have the freedom to hold even incorrect understanding of scriptural truth until genuinely convinced otherwise.

4) Believers should be able to function in union holding in tandem both truth and freedom.

Discussion Questions

1) What do you think of the idea that the unique environment of America in the 1800's gave birth to the Stone-Campbell Movement? What aspects of American life might have contributed to its birth besides those mentioned? If a new Thomas Campbell were to emigrate to America today, what different aspects of current American life might enhance founding a similar movement? How might it be different? The same?

2) One of the continuing American cultural values is Locke's principle of tolerance. We even continue to use the word. What are some specific examples on how America has failed in that principle? Excelled?

What are some areas you see the need for more tolerance? Less?

3) Besides "no creed but Christ," what are some truths from Scripture that all Christians and all Churches should hold? Where are they found in Scripture?

4) What are some examples of beliefs held as scriptural truth in your congregation that other congregations or denominations should not be required to hold in order to be considered fellow Christians?

5) What are some examples of beliefs you personally hold to be scriptural truth that others in your congregation or other believers generally should not be required to hold?

6) When you meet people who you recognize to be a fellow Christian, how might you go about having a conversation with them about what you hold in common? Or matters you don't hold in common?

7) In your opinion, can truth and freedom be held in tandem? How do you personally apply this to yourself? Is this idea just too idealistic?

NOTES

NOTES

Leader's Notes

Leader's Notes

Lesson #1: Lordship of Jesus Christ

Question 1. The practice of allowing only members of a particular Christian congregation, sect or denomination, rather than all believers in Christ to share in the Lord's Supper is known as "close Communion." Early Restoration Movement leaders rejected close Communion, asserting that the Supper is "the *Lord's* Supper" (I Corinthians 11:20), and they were not capable of judging another's right to a place at the table. Perhaps they deemed it more offensive to exclude one from the Supper who really did belong to the Lord than to participate occasionally with someone who might be insincere.

One of the problems with creeds or humanly devised confessions of faith is that they are particular, not universal. Alexander Campbell, in a debate with N. L. Rice in 1843 dealing in part with creeds, stated, "A creed or confession of faith is an ecclesiastic document—*the mind and will of some synod or council possessing authority*—as a term of communion, by which persons and opinions are to be tested, approbated, or reprobated" (emphasis added). Creeds are statements of what a particular group of people at certain times *thought* the Scriptures meant. Because these confessions are authoritative for the denominations that produced them, creeds, not Scripture, became the means of testing believers' beliefs and faith. So, some might be faithful to Scripture and to the Lord but judged unworthy because they are out of step with the denomination's creed.

Question 2. People may acknowledge Jesus to be Lord of his or her life, state their intention to obey His will and still be ignorant or wrong about some teachings of the New Testament. Does an error in understanding a doctrine keep believers from having Jesus as Lord? No. In Proposition 6 of the *Declaration and Address,* Thomas Campbell wrote,

> That although inferences and deductions from scripture premises, when fairly inferred, may be truly called the doctrine of God's holy word, yet are they not formally binding upon the consciences of Christians farther than they perceive the connection, and evidently see that they are so; for their faith must not stand in the wisdom of men; but in the power and veracity of God. Therefore, no such deduction can be made terms of communion, but do properly belong to the after and progressive edification of the Church. Hence, it is evident that no such deductions or inferential truths ought to have any place in the Church's confession.

Salvation does not depend upon the ability to understand meaning of Scripture, nor to discover truth by the power of deductive reasoning (learning from general to specific ideas), but upon agreement to the clear acknowledgement that Jesus "is the Christ, the son of the living God" (Matthew 16:16).

Question 3. Some have used the word "boss" as a synonym for Lord. That certainly communicates the issue of authority, but may fall short of identifying the grace in Jesus' Lordship. Jesus is a unique Master. Setting aside self-interest, He exercises His authority as a servant who is genuinely committed to the success and well being of His loved one. (He did, after all, "lay down his life for his friends.") The leader should communicate the marvelous blend of authority and grace in Jesus' Lordship that is all too rare in our experience of human authority.

Question 4. Don't let the group evade this issue by settling for generalities. At *Hope*, we teach that another way of understanding salvation is becoming a party of the New Covenant with God through Christ. Covenants involve terms that the partners with God pledge to observe. We teach that the two major terms of the New Covenant are helping others be reconciled to God and disciplining our lives to grow into Christlikeness. It might help the group to be specific about responding to Jesus' Lordship by considering decisions and relationships in light of these terms.

Question 5. There are two important issues to keep in mind about the church's experience of the Lord's Supper. First, the Lord's Supper, or Communion, is a corporate, not private event. Believers at the table do not shut everything and everyone else out and pretend they are alone with the Lord. Believers respond to Jesus' Lordship as members of a Body that encourages them in and holds them accountable for their daily obedience to Christ. The whole Body has a stake in each member's success or failure in faithfulness.

Second, the Lord's Supper is a moment of covenant renewal. We bring deliberately and vividly to mind our earlier pledge to yield to Jesus and share His mission. William Robinson, a respected scholar in the British Churches of Christ, wrote in *The Biblical Doctrine of the Church* that the church is the continuation or extension of the Incarnation (Jesus the Word of God in flesh). The Lord continues to do through the church what He did on earth in the flesh. Keeping this in mind, we might find it easier to imagine where we are succeeding and where we need repenting during our covenant renewal at Communion.

Question 6. There is not always a precise method prescribed in the New Testament for accomplishing the Lord's commands and commission. Many in the Restoration Movement have thought it acceptable to employ strategies and methods facilitating implementation of the Lord's will, even if such teachings are not commanded in the New Testament. These may be helpful and are permissible when they assist in doing what God wants but should be rejected when they go against it. Examples of helpful activities are Sunday (Bible) School, musical instruments accompanying worship, association of churches devoted to supporting mission, or the invitation hymn at the close of corporate worship, to name but a few. These are not mandated in Scripture. Problems arise when familiar helpful activities are elevated to the level of requirements in the church's "unwritten creed." Attempts to eliminate or change any helpful activities for the sake of following Scripture or Christ may be met with resistance. The question is: lacking a "thus saith the Lord" for a practice, are we flexible enough to change or even dispense with strategies and methods when change best serves the Lord's purpose?

Question 7. In Colossians 1:28, Paul uses the Greek word *teleion* to describe what we are in Christ. The word means mature, complete or perfect. Paul is declaring that we find completion as human beings in unity with Christ. Our acknowledgment that Jesus Christ is Lord is admission that shows Jesus as the true model of undefiled humanity. Jesus saves us, not only by going to the cross on our behalf, but also by demonstrating in His perfection the nature of the humanity God intended at creation. This provides us with the image of our recreated lives. Enticed by many options, we submit to *Him alone* as the appropriate model for our humanity. At conversion God forgives our sin and regards us as the perfect humanity He intended. We spend all the remaining time of our lives becoming, in fact, how God already sees us in Christ.

Lesson #2: The Authority of Scripture

Question 1. Dr. North clearly identifies the difficulty of people with different theologies. The more intellectually and emotionally tied to one's interpretation of Scripture, the stronger the commitment to the truth of the viewpoints will be. Thomas and Alexander Campbell held to the common view of Postmillennialism because they thought that America was the heart of where the truth of God's word was ultimately going to mature. The very name – *The Millennial Harbinger* – declared that point of view. In the 21st century Restoration churches, the Premillennial view of Biblical interpretation has now become a dominant view. How can those who hold either view so strongly trust the teachings of the other? Where is the common ground to be found? In my early years, I was taught and accepted that the only true name for the church was "Christian Church." It was truly the non-denominational name and was handed down from the early church. Restoring the church meant restoring the true name. Even attending or associating with persons who worshipped in Lutheran or Baptist churches was frowned on. Only later did someone teach me that "Church of God" or "Assembly of God" were biblical as well. What are the essentials (the bene esse) of faith that believers hold to be accepted as brothers and sisters in Christ?

Question 2. When we make a claim that we are people who accept the Bible "as our only rule of faith and practice," what are we saying? If I assert that the Bible is the inerrant, infallible Word of God while suggesting that not every story in the Old or New Testament must be accepted as truth, have I falsified the "only rule of faith and practice" commitment generally taught in the RM? Suppose one, like Luther, denied that the book of James should be a part of the New Testament, can that person remain true to the Bible?

The term "Open Theology" has only recently been added to my vocabulary and I have been asked about my opinion on its truth or viable way of interpreting the concept of "foreknowlege." In my formative years, I was taught to reject Calvin's predestination because surely didn't decide beforehand who was going to save or not save. Freewill allow all to choose for themselves. However, I was advised that God's foreknowledge did cause Him to know who would ultimately be saved even if he had predestined it. God knew all outcomes in His all-knowing powers. Is someone who holds that God may not know the outcomes of all things and even may somehow or sometimes change His mind still capable of being a part of the body of Christ to which I am called and view myself as a member? Would this fall into the essential nature of belief that suggests that one is or is not a fellow citizen of the kingdom and a part of the body of Christ?

Question 3. So, if Dr. North has raised a vital question that forces one to choose sides on how we are going to separate believers and non-believers, have we reached an unsolvable question/issue that means Christian unity as taught in the RM must be rejected? Or are they the wrong standards to establish as the basis of Christian unity?

Suppose we were to accept a different starting point for the discussion? Suppose we were to look at one's relationship to Jesus Christ as our Savior and his life as our only standard of faith and practice as ultimate truth that binds Christians together, that views of other theologies and ideals are all non-essentials, would it then be possible to have a unified church on early? Does that destroy our basic value on the Scriptures since it contains our primary source about Jesus Christ as Lord and Savior?

Lesson #3: Unity of Christians

Question 1. It is inevitable that most churches will experience severe and divisive conflict at some point in their history. It might be worthwhile here to have the study group explore the various causes of those conflicts in which they have personally been involved. Point out passages in the New Testament that bear witness to conflict among Christians, and have the group identify the defining issues involved (Acts 6:1-6; 15:36-41; I Corinthians 1:10-17; Philippians 4:2-3; I John 2:18-19; II John 7-11; III John 9-10). The last three passages are particularly relevant since they are addressed to the same historical community as the Gospel of John. It seems that the unity for which Jesus prayed was undergoing severe testing by the time the letters of John were written.

Question 2. Denominations can be helpful if they are seen as dialects of the same language. In that case they add their own distinct voices to the way the church speaks as a whole. The minute denominations assume the essence of church, however, and limit their fellowship around the table only to their own members, they become occasions for sinful division in the church. This was the denominational world of nineteenth-century America into which the Stone-Campbell Movement was born. Thomas Campbell got into trouble not long after coming to America, because he actually had the "audacity" to share Communion with Presbyterians who were not of his particular Presbytery! Perhaps a quick poll of the denominational backgrounds represented in your study group can determine to what extent these kinds of narrow-minded attitudes still exist today among denominations and groups.

Question 3. The way in which the Letter to the Ephesians speaks of unity as both a present reality and a future goal is worthy of sustained reflection. "Unity of the Spirit" could be understood as unity *from* the Spirit, emphasizing the Spirit as the source from which our unity derives. If the Spirit is the author of our unity, then unity is not dependent upon human ingenuity or achievement. We are simply to maintain or keep what the Spirit has already given. At the same time, Christ has given various offices to the church (apostles, prophets, evangelists, etc.) for the equipping of believers for the work of ministry and the building up of the body of Christ (church), the result of which is a practical growth towards unity of faith and knowledge. In this way the church is to work *practically* towards that which it already is *positionally* in Christ.

Question 4. The presence of the Greek article with the term "faith" in verse 13 ("the faith") suggests that a body of doctrine is in view here rather than an act of personal trust in Christ. Unity of the faith is thus closely linked with growth in knowledge and maturity. It is important to realize that we are saved not by how much knowledge we attain but by grace (Ephesians 2:8-10), and that Christians will differ in their knowledge of Christ depending on their level of maturity. If we only have fellowship with "mature" Christians, we will deprive one another of mutual teaching and learning opportunities in our common quest for greater Christlikeness.

Question 5. Christians sometimes forget that unity is part of the truth Christ gave us. Each Christian has a responsibility to "maintain the unity of the Spirit" (Ephesians 4:3) while "speaking the truth in love" (Ephesians 4:15). Jesus desired the unity of the church (John 17:20-23), as well as its guidance into all the truth (John 16:13). But how can we have unity with someone we perceive to be "in error"? If unity is understood as insistence on doctrinal conformity, then unity will be difficult to achieve indeed, as the history of the church demonstrates so sadly but so well. But if unity consists in common allegiance to a Person, then the unity of the Spirit can exist despite our differences.

Question 6. Determining what is "essential" to the faith is the $64,000 question. What seems so clearly to be an essential to one person may not seem so clear to another. Take the Trinity, for example. Most Christians today would consider the co-eternality of the Father, Son, and Holy Spirit ("three-in-one") to be an essential of the faith. Yet Barton Stone and Alexander Campbell disagreed on this issue, with Stone denying the co-eternality of the Son and Campbell affirming it through the identification of Jesus as the "Word" of God. Or take the issue of the substitutionary atonement of Christ, which most Christians today assume is an essential of the faith. While both Stone and Campbell believed that the death of Jesus cleanses us from sin, they did not agree on the manner in which it does so. The remarkable thing is that Campbell and Stone could debate these issues from the Scriptures without calling into question each other's relationship to Jesus! In pointing out this remarkable toleration of views to members of your study group, some may express surprise at just how far our founders were willing to go to preserve the unity of the church.

Question 7a. The issue of speaking in tongues has divided many a church. Some Christians argue that the gift of tongues that existed in the first century (I Corinthians 12:4-11; 14:1-19) exists today and should be exercised in the Body of Christ. Others believe that the gift of tongues ceased with the apostles (I Corinthians 13:8-12) and no longer has a place in the life of the church. Poll the members of your group to see what they think about the gifts of the Spirit. Ask them to come up with a policy that would respect their differences and still maintain the unity of the church.

Questions 7b,c,d. These scenarios involve some of the most controversial social and political issues of our day. They are intended to be provocative and generate discussion in an effort to see just how serious we are about unity and how far we are willing to take it. It is one thing for a Christian to affirm unity when *his* issue is not at stake; it is quite another for a Christian to affirm unity when an issue she regards as essential or true is not shared by other Christians. These issues should help clarify just how "big" the church really is in the thinking of your study group.

Lesson #4: Covenant in the Restoration Tradition

Question 1. The Hebrew term "barith" means "to cut" and refers to the blood sacrifice often made in ratifying a treaty. The Hebrew term "hesed" was sometimes translated "mercy" or "loving kindness" or "faithfulness" and meant to return good for good received—gratitude. In the New Covenant, our new treaty with God has been ratified through the blood sacrifice of Jesus demonstrating God's great love for humankind (Romans 5:8). The equivalent of "hesed" in the New Testament is the gratitude (agape love) we show by serving each other and our world. This is true worship. Jesus is the end of all the Old Testament sacrifices except the "thank" offering. These offerings God now desires from us as cited in Romans 12:1-2, 15:7, 16; Hebrews 13:15. 13:16.

Question 2. Use the chart to compare covenants. Have participants share examples of how one might think and act during the Old Covenant compared to thinking and behavior in the New Covenant times.

Question 3. Hebrews chapters 3-12 shows how, in many ways, Jesus and the New Covenant are superior to the Old. **Jesus** is superior: as Savior and High Priest--chapters 2, 3 and to Moses--chapters 3, 4. **Jesus** offers: a superior Priesthood--chapters 4, 5, 7; a superior Sacrifice--chapters 8, 9, 10; and superior rewards--chapters 11, 12. The law could not make anyone good (righteousness). Jesus frees us from sin and death and empowers us to live good and holy lives (Romans 8)

Question 4. We are not under any law except the law of Love. Love (hesed) covers everything God intended to make a part of the New Covenant. Read: Romans 13:8-14; John

13:34, 15:12-17; Matthew 22:34-40; James 2:8-13; I John 4:7-21.

Question 5. Draw a circle. The outside edge represents a legal based religious code. A religion based on "do nots" creates a preoccupation with the negative. Now put "Christlikeness" and "Love" in the middle of the circle. Focus on the center will pull us away from the edge. Life is no longer reactive but proactive (Philippians 4:4-9; Romans 6:11-23, 8:12-16; Galatians 6:2; I Corinthians 9:21; James 2:8).

Question 6. Bringing into the New Covenant those laws that were intended for the nation of Israel creates a return to "legalism." For instance, the bringing forward of Jewish festivals, Sabbath laws, special sacrifices, food laws, etc. all create a legal code similar to that from which we have been set free (Colossians 2:12-23). To be obliged to keep one part of the old law is obligation to keep it all (Galatians 3:1-5, 18-29, 5:1-6).

Some Christians do the following in legalistic manner: church order of worship, use of alcohol, dancing, gambling, smoking, etc. The group might add to this list. Some preachers imply that God desires each Christian to prosper materially. While the New Testament does teach that God will give back to us more than we give (Luke 6:34-38; 12:15), it does not say it will be a financial reward on earth. Rather, we are to lay up "treasures in heaven" (Matthew 6:19-21; I Timothy 6:17-19).

Question 7. One entered the Old Covenant through birth. Keeping that covenant was to obey the 613 laws given to Moses. Provision was made for minor breaking of the commands, but abandonment of the covenant meant that the covenant was no longer in effect. A husband and wife enter into the marriage covenant through the making of public and legal pledges. Keeping the marriage contract is different than entering into it. Similarly, the New Covenant is entered into through faith in Christ demonstrated in baptism and repentance. Keeping the covenant carries with it obligations to strive to grow into Christlikeness and to help our new Master succeed in His mission. Provision is also made for minor breaches (I John 1:9), but abandonment of the covenant is abandonment of God. As in marriage, the abandoned party is not forced to keep his or her vows if the other partner abandons the contract (Hebrews 6:1-6; I Corinthians 7:15).

Question 8. God has designed us so that we desire to return good for good received. The action of God in Christ is so great that it puts us under moral obligation to show gratitude (praise). We are told the converts on Pentecost were cut to the heart and cried out, "what shall we do?" The story of the cross "cuts us to the heart" as well and awakens in us the desire to turn from our old direction and towards God. The story of the cross demands that we live lives of thankfulness and service for what He has done for us.

Lesson #5 Mission and World Evangelism

Question 1: As the loving family of the future missionary, we have a responsibility to partner with the person doing the going. There are New Testament examples of congregations coming alongside fellow workers in the field. The church at Antioch received word directly from the Holy Spirit concerning setting aside Barnabas & Saul to be sent out as missionaries (Acts 13:1-3). After they had prayed and fasted, they placed their hands on Barnabas and Saul, indicating their blessing, and sent them off. Paul later wrote to the Romans, letting them know of his plans to visit Spain, stopping off to see them so they could assist him on his journey (Romans 15:23-24).

The command to go in the Great Commission (Matthew 28:18-20) is accompanied by multiple examples in the New Testament of caring for those going. Matthew 10 sees Jesus sending His disciples off to preach and expecting hospitality to be shown to them. Luke 8:1-3 sets the pattern of support in Jesus' life and ministry as well. Jesus traveled; his disciples and others were with him, and He allowed others to share their goods with the group.

In these passages and many more, we see the need for praying for and blessing with materials goods those who are going from our midst to share the gospel with others. Discuss with the group what their ideas are for partnering with new missionaries from within their midst and how those ideas might be accomplished. Some questions to consider include: How can we help in confirming a person's missionary calling and gifting for intercultural ministry? How can we help in providing the training needed to serve as an intercultural missionary? How can we stretch our faith by committing to be partners with our resources? How can we send them out with our blessing?

Question 2: This question has been debated over the centuries among many denominations. The trend among Protestants from the 1500s to the 1700s was to leave people alone, thinking that as long as they had not heard the Good News, they would not have to be responsible to God. When William Carey, the Father of modern Protestant missions, announced his decision to become a missionary to India in 1792 at a minister's meeting, he was met with the rebuke, "Young man, sit down! If God wants to save the heathen he will do it without your help or mine."

In a postmodern, post-Christian society, we are more likely to hear folks say, "Let people find their own way to God, by their own path." While it is clearly possible that God can be revealed to people through their own understandings, and even through nature (Romans 1:18-20), we cannot ignore the message we have received through the Scriptures, that Jesus is the one way to God (John 14:6). He is not one way among many, but the only way.

Jesus gives us a clear understanding of our responsibility in the process when in Matthew 28:19 He says, "Go, and make disciples of all nations." That theme of all nations is echoed in Acts 1:8, as Jesus told His followers that they would be His witnesses first in Jerusalem, then Judea and Samaria, and to the ends of the earth.

With the group, look at a world map, noting how the church started in Jerusalem, and then spread out around the world from there. Concentric rings are formed starting at Jerusalem and spreading out to the rest of the world like ripples spreading on a pond. We are called to cross boundaries (social, linguistic, ethnic, religious...) and proclaim the message of the good news of the Kingdom of God. It is becoming increasingly true that Christians around the world are continuing in the missionary task, even if churches in the West are not... God's mission might be accomplished without your help or mine, but God's desire, clearly seen in the Bible, is that we join in God's mission as witnesses for Jesus!

Question 3: The Jerusalem church was comfortable in their homogeneity as Jewish background believers in Jesus. However, when Peter visited Cornelius (Acts 10) and was given a vision from God, the church in Jerusalem was challenged to rethink their exclusive relationship with God as well as special traditions they were following (Acts 11:18). Revelation 7:9 paints a beautiful picture of people from every tribe, language and nation praising God around the throne. With people of every ethnic group living near us today, this picture also presents a clear challenge to us to diversify our church ministries in the community.

Poll the members of your group to find out what ethnic groups are living in their neighborhoods today. How have those changed in the last few years? What about your church and even your group? Is it representative of those groups? Reaching out across cultural barriers usually takes motivation, training and intentional effort. Discuss how this current challenge might be met by your church.

Can your church consider participating in ministry to immigrants and refugees in your community? Remember, God loves the alien (Deut. 10.14-19; Psalm 146.6-9; Jeremiah 7.4-8; Zech. 7.8-10), and in God's eyes, we were all once aliens and separated from God until we understood the salvation offered through faith in Jesus.

Question 4: By staying active in studying the Scripture we can avoid straying from the Scripture. Just as John urged his readers to "test the spirits to see whether they are from God" (1 John 4:1), those who share Christ across cultural boundaries must constantly test their words and actions to see if they are from God and are following the biblical lines. Paul wrote to Timothy admonishing him to present himself as one who "correctly handles the word of truth" (2 Timothy 2:15). That must be the effort of everyone who works cross-culturally, whether it is on a local or global level.

We must also remember that for those who have accepted the message of Jesus in other cultures, the Holy Spirit is also guiding and directing them as they study the Scriptures. Together, both missionaries and local church leaders, through prayer, study of the Bible, and close examination of the meaning of cultural practices, can make the best decisions regarding diverse cultural practices.

Question 5: As a group, or in small groups if your group is large, discuss and make a list of what is considered to be essential for worship. While people have a tendency to be tied very emotionally to their comfortable worship styles, remember that not every picture of worship in the New Testament is an exact mirror image of the others. Why? The answer is because different people from different locations were taking part in that worship. Generational differences and regional differences show up readily in the worship styles of services across America. Some want to worship early in the morning, while others are more comfortable with a midday service. Some desire an organ playing, while others find comfort in no instruments or multiple instruments.

The first church was pictured as meeting together daily, praying, studying the Word, fellowshipping, breaking bread and sharing all their material possessions (Acts 2:42-47). How well to our churches match this example of daily "lived" worship? If these elements are included, is there flexibility concerning other cultural parts of the service?

Question 6: While the evangelization of the world is everyone's responsibility and since we all received the mandate from Jesus to "Go and make disciples" (Matthew 28:18-20), how that is going to look in everyone's life is different. Each of us has been given different gifts and different callings. Some are called to be apostles, some pastors, some teachers and all for the building up of the church (2 Corinthians 12:12-31). Discuss what each person's call is and how he or she might live toward that call.

While all of us are called to be witnesses, not all of us are called to full-time ministry in the church or to serve as boundary-crossing intercultural missionaries. If someone in your group or congregation is feeling God's calling to serve in these ways, it is your responsibility as part of the community to pray and seek confirmation for your sister or brother's calling.

Lesson #6: The Priesthood of All Believers

Question 1: The image of the priest can denote many things to different people. For those who have grown up in a more liturgical tradition (Roman Catholic, Episcopalian, etc.) they may see a priest as the one in authority who conducts the service. One might associate robes or other clerical vestments with this role.

In the Old Testament, priests were often pictured as descendents of Aaron. The practiced many religious services such as reciving tithes, worshipping God, offering sacrifices and prayer for the people. The role of the high priest was to offer sins on behalf of the entire nation of Israel through a once-a-year sacrifice in the temple that made atonement for the sins of himself and the people that had been committed through the year.

In the New Testament, Jesus is seen as the high priest (see Hebrews 5-10) who makes atonement for the sins of all and opens up the way for all to know and follow God. In the New Testament, there also isn't a role of priest mentioned as part of Christian worship, but rather it opens up the idea that all can participate and connect with God through Jesus Christ.

Question 2: The Revelation passage may harken back to Exodus 19:6 which states "but you shall be for me a priestly kingdom and a holy nation." The nation of Israel as a people were not meant to be a blessed people to keep it to themselves. Instead, they were blessed so that all nations would be blessed through them (Gen 12:1-3). Our job then as a priesthood of believers is not to be a people who are somehow superior or more devout, but rather to bless others through the good news and action of Jesus Christ.

Likewise, 1 Peter 2:9 declares that the priesthood is not a special class of people, but all of God's people who are called to proclaim the good news of being called out of darkness and into the light.

Question 3: As the verse from 1 Cor 12 above states, each has his or her own job or role, but we are all a part of the priesthood. Discuss a bit how you fit into this priesthood, and how the career or calling that you feel in your life is a part of the larger body of Christ. Also, discuss how you feel the job or career that you have can be done in a way that expresses worship to God.

Question 4: Are there people in your local church body who are overlooked or not used? In many churches, we put a high value on gifting that are used in front of other people (preaching, teaching, worship leading, etc.). However, there are many who have gifts that go unseen. When you think about the church community you are a part of, how can you help enable that all are using their gifts? Think through specific ways to empower others in their gifting, or perhaps even discover what they are.

Question 5: This question jumps off from the last question. The idea of this verse is not that each person in the body has one of the specific gifting mentioned in this passage. Instead the church, or the body of Christ, needs people with a variety of skills, talents, and occupations to serve within the local congregation and just as importantly beyond the church walls. When we think of the analogy of the body, there are many parts indeed, each with its own function. How do they all fit together? Think of examples of gifting or service that are needed within a local church congregation.

Question 6: When we begin to think of the church as a priesthood of all believers, it may change our image of what the role of the local church is. No longer do we need to see the local church as the way that we hear a message or word from God. Instead, we are all "the church" and are therefore those who are called to dispense the good news of Jesus to the entire world in a variety of ways. The local church congregation then becomes a way for us to celebrate what God has done in our lives, be discipled, prepare to go and share with the world and be a location where needs can be met. There may be other purposes of the local church also. Can you think of any?

Question 7: This is an important question, particularly for those who have grown up in the church and may not view the church this way. How does the idea of being a priest challenge you to live differently? This should change our notion of church, as mentioned in question 6 also. We are all "the church" and it is not something we go to, but rather an identity of those who follow Jesus Christ and have our lives changed by him. What changes does this necessitate?

Lesson #7: Servant Leadership

Question 1: The answer to this question is subjective. However, there are some objective definitions that can be referred to. Donald Nash in his book *Word Pictures* (p. 163) discusses six words that are translated as servant in the New Testament. Along with a brief definition they are: doulos – an absolute slave; therapon (therapy which helps heal) - one who serves out of love and duty; diakonos (term we get minister and deacon from) – one who will run through the dust; oiketes – a favored servant in the household; uperetes – a menial servant willing to serve even to the point of death; pais –the adult who serves the child whom he loves. Each of these words gives a partial idea of what it is to serve.

Leadership is very big today. Many books have been and are being written on the subject. Simply, leadership is **influence.** When a person influences another person, a group of people, or an organization, he or she is leading. When vision, directions, and actions occur, leadership is the impetus. Servants can lead. Leaders would be wise to serve.

Question 2: The tension of this question is the result of our common definitions of terms and the culture in which we live. Leaders are usually perceived as controllers and tellers. Servants are usually controlled and told.

Upon reflection, however, almost everyone can think of a person in authority who is respected or loved because he or she cares and does something for others on their level or for them personally. A loving mother leads and teaches her children. What endears her to her children is her care, concern, compassion, sacrifice and selflessness.

There is a positional power and personal power. Positional power comes from having a place of authority. Personal power is the result of interpersonal relationship. There is a bond between the people. The leader who not only has power due to his or her position, but also because of a personal relationship, usually has more influence upon one's followers.

Question 3: Many people think the culture of their workplace would not be open to serving. Grabbing authority and power struggles are the normal actions. Perhaps this pessimism is due to an unrealistic view that the whole organization is never going to adopt the servant attitude. They may feel they do not have enough influence to make such a broad, drastic change. And they may be correct.

However, every person can bloom where he/she is planted. A worker can influence and serve those immediately around him/her. That area is a realistic place to start. As leaven influences the whole loaf of bread, a small start may work its way through the whole organization.

Question 4: Hopefully, there are many answers given. Ideally, there are no power-hungry people in the church. Most churches have unsung heroes who work in the nursery, clean the kitchen, care for the plants, prepare communion, make phone calls, pray, etc.

This question is a good time to reflect on those who give a "cup of water" in Jesus' name! Have each person give themselves and others credit for the small works that they do. These small works have more effect then one realizes.

Question 5: The focus of these questions starts at, but goes beyond, church involvement. The family, work, volunteer organizations, etc. should be explored. The church needs to recognize that ministry goes beyond the organized church. When the church serves in the community ministry is taking place. A person serving a PTA is doing ministry. A person being a crossing guard is doing ministry. The church members' service outside of the organized church needs to be affirmed as being legitimate servant leadership ministry.

How can a person grow? Only they can tell us. Encourage the group to take incremental steps. Growth is a process. It takes time. Encourage them to rejoice in each step.

Question 6: There is no right answer to this series of questions. There are obvious people like Mother Theresa. Many famous people may be mentioned. However, other historical people may be deceased family members or friends who impacted their life or the lives of others.

Hopefully, the discussion lends itself to see how these people influenced others by guiding and caring for them. Perhaps the family, business, church, city, state, country, or even the world is different because of these historical figures! See if there is a common theme as to why these people were mentioned.

Question 7: As the focus of the previous question is upon historical people, the focus of this question is upon contemporary people. These are people they know now. The context may be family, business, church or the community.

Hopefully the discussion lends itself to see how these people influence others by guiding and caring for them. Again, listen for common themes of the kind of people mentioned (mothers, teachers, preachers) or the characteristics these people demonstrated.

Question 8: Refer back to the texts mentioned in the body of the lesson. Discuss some of them. Point out Jesus' consistent attitude and behavior to really care for others. This care sometimes included "tough love" and confrontation.

Ask the group if they can think of other incidents in Jesus' life in addition to the texts listed.

Question 9: Usually fear is the roadblock to belief and practice. There can be a fear of success (expectation) to live this concept out, or there may be a fear of failure. Some will fear that it will make no difference. Others fear not knowing what to do.

Explore the groups' fears and inquire about steps to overcome those fears. Some helps are: prayer, education, group support, mentoring and the freedom to experience the truth of servant leadership.

Lesson # 8: The Church

Question 1: Spend some time discussing perceptions of the church which group members have encountered in their interactions with non church-attending family members, friends, co-workers, and neighbors. Have them also discuss what they have heard in the popular media about the church. Based on these insights discuss whether or not they agree with the idea that the perceived value of the church as an institution is in decline in our society today. Then take a few minutes to explore perceptions of the church among active church-goers. Have they encountered doubts about the value of the church even among engaged Christians? If so what are some of the reasons for this?

Question 2: Contemporary American society seems to be busier than ever, with increasing demands upon our time and resources. Many activities even seem to offer alternative options for experiencing "community" – a popular buzzword not only in the church but also in the society around us. What this suggests is that people are yearning for meaningful connections with others and are searching for opportunities to experience this. Discuss with the group some of the alternatives for "fellowship" that our society offers to us. Have them then consider what the church can learn from these other types of fellowship. In other words, how do these alternative institutions offer something of value to their participants? To conclude this question, have the group discuss the ways in which the fellowship of the church is different from these alternatives. What value does the church offer that these other institutions do not? What is superior about the fellowship that the church has to offer?

Question 3 and 4: For many Christians, particularly those who are young in faith, the fact that there are different churches on nearly every street corner is a disconcerting observation which raises a number of difficult questions. "How do I know that 'my' church is the 'right' one?" "Why can't these churches get along?" "Wouldn't they accomplish a lot more if they worked together?" "If Christians are always talking about love, why does there seem to be so much division and disagreement between them?" These are important questions, but it is vital to remember that even though there are many different Christian denominations this does not necessarily mean that there is animosity or competition among them. Rather, much of the denominational variety in the church today is a result of things that might be termed "non-essential," for example, theological differences on specific issues, preferences for a particular style of worship, or ethnic, cultural, and language differences. A Christian may choose to be a member of a particular local church for a variety of reasons but should also recognize that he or she is part of the Body of Christ at-large and is therefore in communion with Christians of all different varieties. As your group discusses this question, have them first identify the essential beliefs and practices that all Christians share. These are things that unify us as Christians. Remind them also that the shorter the list of essentials, the greater the possibility for Christian unity will be. Following this, have them then discuss practical ways in which their church can express unity with Christians of other denominations and congregations.

Question 5: The fundamental distinction of the church, which makes its fellowship unique as compared with other types of human institutions, is that God has called the church to be engaged in the ministry of reconciliation (2 Corinthians 5:11-6:10), which has as its goal restoring the relationship between God and sinful humanity. As a result, there is more at stake in Christian fellowship than simply enjoying one another's company, as valuable and worthwhile as this may be. Christian service has an eternal significance as we work according to the values of the Kingdom of God. One of the important contributions of the Stone-Campbell movement was an emphasis on the concept of the "priesthood of all believers," the idea that every Christian has a vital role to play in the church's mission. As you discuss this question, have participants talk about the ways in which the church has helped them to find their spiritual gifts, has helped to equip them for Christian service, and has given them opportunities to serve.

Lesson #9: Freedom of Interpretation

Question 1. One prominent aspect of early American life is individualism and self-improvement. Think of Benjamin Franklin's *Poor Richard's Almanac* and its early and influence. Think of self-made people, who made choices to improve themselves and their lot in life by hard work and perseverance. Think of people moving West (Western Pennsylvania is the frontier in Thomas Campbell's day). Think of people trying to start their lives over from scratch. This all contributes to the idea of starting over with the church or with one's faith as Thomas and Alexander Campbell wanted to do. Think of the right to vote then (for men, anyway). This was new. Think of the emphasis on education. This all leads to thinking for oneself, reading the Bible for oneself, and develop individual interpretation and opinions.

What about Thomas Campbell coming here today? He would see freedom of interpretation expressed everywhere. From blogs, to texts to tweets, and whatever new social media trend that may extend from these. What if he were to have blog? Or a personal website? What might he do with these opportunities? On the other hand, would he find the traffic of opinion so overloaded that he could not get a large hearing and eventual following? Consider have a class dialogue about these possibilities.

Question 2. The idea of tolerance remains embedded in American culture. However, the principle runs a tenuous course through American history and still today. Open this section of questions with a discussion regarding how "tolerance" crops up in political and social dialogue and reporting regarding issues today. On the first question regarding "has failed," probe issues of the past like persecution of various religious groups, like Mormons, or prejudice against ethnic groups like the Irish when they first arrived, or Asians, Japanese during World War II (internment camps), and certainly African-Americans, and woman (right to vote).

On the second question, "excelled," consider the eventual acceptance or toleration of the groups mentioned in the first question. On the third question of "more tolerance" today, reflect on the backlash of intolerance toward conservative evangelical Christians, prayer in schools, or other civic events. On the fourth question of "less tolerance" today, consider issues like abortion, gay rights, or evolution in schools.

Question 3. The *Declaration and Address* likes to use the word "express" for beliefs that are crystal clear in Scripture, beliefs that all Christians hold to be clear in Scripture. Think about beliefs that might be in basic statements of faith, like: Salvation is only through belief in Christ; Christ died for the sins of the world; Jesus rose from the dead on the third day; Christ will return to judge the world. Jesus is the Chris is the Son of God.

Question 4. Consider beliefs that other congregations and denominations might tend to disagree with yours about: weekly Lord's Supper offered to all present, immersion as the only mode of baptism, and baptism for salvation only for those old enough to possess and express their own personal faith. Maybe your particular congregation (or preaching minister) influences many with some interesting views that might not necessarily need to be held by others.

Question 5. Possibly, that many people cannot answer this because they have not done very much personal study of the Bible. Maybe some in your class believe that the life on earth came to fruition in just 6-days or others that evolution has worked together with God's creation in some way to create the earth and life.

Question 6. As the leader, maybe you can provide an example of conversations like this you have had with neighbors or coworkers. Reflect on how you might have been able to go about it better to create more unity out of the diversity or even to have been more genuinely interactive about differences. Maybe you are in an ongoing relationship with someone with whom you might consider a new approach. A general observation is that one could start a conversation asking about the church congregations that the other person associates with, their denomination, and any distinctive beliefs you may already know about.

Question 7. When truth and freedom are not held in tandem, this invites trouble. Truth with no freedom creates legalism, arrogance, distant relationships. Freedom without truth creates universalism, (meaning all are saved regardless of their religion or lack of any religion or faith). Freedom and truth have to be held together. In terms of your own practice (or anyone's), it is true that speeding can lead to fatal accidents, yet most of us assert our freedom by always or occasionally driving in excess of the posted speed limits. It is also true that smoking (and other habits) is detrimental to our health, yet people exercise their freedom to continue those habits. Think along those lines to begin sharing.

To hold truth and freedom perfectly in tandem is probably not usually achievable, but as a life practice it is generally a good idea.

Additional Resources

Restoration Movement and the Independent Christian Churches/ Church of Christ

Campbell, Alexander. The Christian System. Gospel Advocate Co., 2001. Available Online: Forrester and Campbell, 1939. http://www.mun.ca/rels/restmov/texts/acampbell/tcs2/TCS200A.HTM.

Campbell, Thomas. Declaration and Address of the Christian Association of Washington. Printed by Brown & Sample, 1809. Available online: http://www.mun.ca/rels/restmov/texts/tcampbell/da/DA1ST.HTM.

Fife, Robert O. Conveying the Incarnation. [Westwood Christian Foundation], c1993

Ford, Harold W. A History of the Restoration Plea: Being a History of the Statements of the Plea of the Churches of Christ for Christian Unity Upon the Basis of a Restoration of the Church of the New Testament. College Press, c1952.

Foster, Douglas A., et al. The Encyclopedia of the Stone-Campbell Movement: Christian Church (Disciples of Christ), Christian Churches/Churches of Christ, Churches of Christ. W.B. Eerdmans Pub., c2004.

Garret, Leroy. The Stone-Campbell Movement: the Story of the American Restoration Movement. Coolege Press Pub. Co.; Rev./Exp.ed., 1994.

"Independent Christian Churches/Church of Christ ."
        Wikipedia.
        http://en.wikipedia.org/wiki/Independant_Christian_C
        hurches/Churches_of_Christ

Knowles, Victor. Together in Christ: More than a Dream.
        College Press, 2006.

Murch, James DeForest. Christians Only: A History of the
        Restoration   Movement.   Wipf   &Stock,   2004.
        Previously published by Standard Publishing, 1962.

Richardson, William J., ed. Christian Docterine: "The Faith,
        Once Delivered." Wipf &Stock, 2004. Previously
        published by Standard Pub., c1983.

Robinson, William. The Biblical Doctrine of the Church.
        Wipf & Stock, [1998?]. Previously published by
        Bethany Press, 1948.

Staton, Knofel. The Paraphrase of Thomas Campbell's
        Declaration and Address (1976) Available Online:
        http://www.mun.ca/rels/restmov/texts/tcampbell/etc/D
        AKS.HTM.

Stone, Sam E. Simply Christians: New Testament Christianity
        in the 21st Century. College Press, c2004.

Stone-Campbell Journal. Semi-annual (April, October).
        Stone-Campbell International. Selections available
        online: http://www.stone-campbelljournal.com

Webb, Henry E. In Search of Christian Unity: A History of
        the Restoration Movement. Standard Pub., c1990.

Welshimer, P.H. Facts Concerning the New Testament
Church (Tracts). Standard Pub., 1996. Available
online:
http://www.burlingtonchristianchurch.org/facts.shtml

Web Sites

Restoration Movement. Hugh and Hazel Darling Library.
Hope International Univerity.
http://library.hiu.edu/majors/rm.html

The Restoration Movement Pages. Maintained by Hans
Rollmann, Memorial University of Newfoundland,
c1995-2004. http://www.mun.ca/rels/restmov/

The Restoration Movement.com. Maintained by Scott Harp.
Fayetteville Church of Christ. Fayetteville, G, c2000.
http://www.therestorationmovement.com/

Stone-Campbell Restoration Resources. Maintained by Jim
McMillan. http://www.bible.acu.edu/stone-campbell/

Advanced Reading

The Restoration Reprint Library. (Over 100 titles reprinted
by College Press.)

The Millennial Harbinger (40 volumes). Edited by Alexander
Campbell and others. Available online:
http://www.mun.ca/rels/restmov/

The Christian Messenger (11 volumes). Edited by Barton
Stone. Available Online:
http://www.mun.ca/rels/restmov/people/bstone.html

For an annotated Version of this list, go to
http://library.hiu.edu/rm_annotated.htm.

About Hope International University

Hope International University (HIU) is a regionally accredited private Christian university encompassing five colleges: College of Arts & Sciences, College of Business & Management, College of Education, Pacific Christian College of Ministry & Biblical Studies, and College of Psychology & Counseling. The institution was founded on October 9, 1928 as Pacific Bible Seminary. In 1930 the seminary moved to Long Beach, and in 1962 the name was changed to Pacific Christian College. When the Long Beach campus was no longer adequate to house the growth of the college, the institution relocated in 1973 to the present campus in Fullerton. In 1997 university status was achieved, and the corporate name was changed to Hope International University.

HIU is a Christian institution of higher learning, rooted in a distinct tradition of service to society through the church. Consequently, the university prepares people for both professional and voluntary leadership in the church and society through undergraduate and graduate degree programs in church ministry, education, business, music, psychology, human development, and other social sciences. Two thirds of Hope's students choose programs delivered via the internet. The university has built the infrastructure and developed a strong track record of delivering online education.

Total university yearly enrollment is approximately 2000 students and an additional 700 students participating in non-degree certificate programs. The student body represents over 35 states and 40 countries.

HIU offers a learning experience that encourages intellectual, social, physical and spiritual development delivered by a faculty and staff dedicated to the learning experience and ultimate success of each graduate. The student to faculty ratio of 16:1 ensures the kind of individualized instruction students need to prepare them for the future. Student life is enhanced through many campus activities including clubs, performing groups, discussion groups, intercollegiate athletic teams and the Associated Student Body. The university is motivated by a very focused mission and is dedicated to empowering students to become servant leaders who will make a difference in the world. Students are encouraged to get involved in church and community service activities, mission trips, tutoring opportunities and intensive internships that give them the kind of foundation necessary to face the challenges of today's world.

Made in the USA
San Bernardino, CA
29 July 2016